Teaching and Learning Materials and the Internet

IAN FORSYTH

KOGAN
PAGE

First published in 1996

Kogan Page Limited
120 Pentonville Road
London N1 9JN

British Library Cataloguing in Publication Data

A CIP record for this book is available from the British Library.

ISBN 0 7494 2059 6

Designed and typeset by N C Murray
Printed and bound in Great Britain by Biddles Ltd, Guildford and King's Lynn

Contents

Preface

Disclaimer

This book is about educational and training course material being delivered using the Internet. It is not about the technical considerations of the Internet, although these are mentioned as needed. For example, it is not my purpose to develop an argument for a particular platform, browser or any other operating system. If I were to do that, I would be offering a snapshot of the Internet as of today's date and some of what I wrote would be out of date as I typed. The information you require for these technical specifications is best found on the Internet at the time you are ready to offer your course. You will note that I use 'the Internet' as a generic term. I find 'World Wide Web' (WWW) or 'surfing the net' to be a problem in education and training terms.

The purpose of this book

This book examines the educational and administration considerations of offering a course, course materials or course delivery via the Internet. While the technical specifications of the capabilities of the Internet will change over time, there is a need to consider course material and the appropriate means of handling it on a delivery mechanism such as the Internet. One of the first considerations is to look for features that indicate the course is relatively stable. If the course material is stable, less course maintenance will be needed. As access to the Internet becomes easier, the features you should be looking for are:

➡ course content should not be volatile, or open to possible changes in the short term;

➡ the appropriate use of technology in relation to access by learners and a consideration of the materials and learning strategies or processes.

There are also educational and training questions raised by the possibility of informal access to your course material by a learner. The Internet is seen as being in the public domain and a learner finding your course material will consider it is available. In other cases, a learner comes across an information site that relates to their work or study. A question needs to be addressed about how the learner gains some sanctioning or accreditation for this informal learning outside a procedural based learning structure or institution providing sanctioned learning.

There are publications on the Internet and in hard copy about the use of the Internet. In most cases this information is about the possibility of achieving the Marshall McLuhan (*The Medium is the Message*) notion of the 'global village' – or is it a village with global access to information? Access to formal education and training on the Internet has a slightly different purpose. In writing this book I have focused on the formal educational and training possibilities available to educators and trainers and learners through the use of the Internet as a means of delivery.

Readers may well ask why I have not used the Internet to publish this book. The explanation is that this *is a book*, not an Internet document. It is a book about the educational use of the Internet. The technology will change and will enhance existing features such as text, file transfer, chat and bulletin boards, graphics and illustrations, audio and video, modelling and virtual reality. It is possible to see how these features can be used for education and training. It is possible to develop instructional design considerations, while the iterations of technology will only make these features more accessible.

If people want to join a discourse on the use of electronic communications there are sites on the Internet. I have created one dealing specifically with the Internet as an instructional design tool.

Ian Forsyth
Sydney, 1996

chapter 1　Preparing Material for the Internet

The Internet is a changing entity. Several years ago the Internet was a computer-based, text-driven communications system for scientists and academics. In the era of the Cold War it was devised to maintain networks if 'The Bomb' was dropped. In the last three years a layer of communications interface called the World Wide Web (WWW) has emerged and with it the use of graphic devices, for point-and-click navigation and an exponential growth of home pages giving access to information ranging from the libraries to parts catalogues. One of the areas for use on the Internet or through WWW is the delivery of educational and training material and the support of education and training.

This summary chapter discusses the four key elements of preparing information for the delivery of educational and training material on the Internet. Figure 1.1 is an indication of the key elements in an Internet page. The content of the figure represents one way of organizing information and this is used in the following figures as a worked example of some ways of navigating material being made available to the learner. This represents a structured approach to learning materials developed by teachers and instructional designers. In part, this summary is designed to show how I would draw together information for a short course on the Internet. Thus it is a model for developing your own course for delivery on the Internet as a course designer. (*Note*: The screen dumps in this publication were developed using Netscape 2.02.)

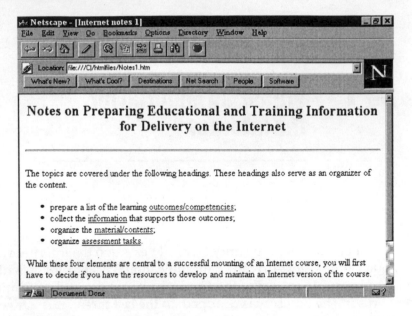

Figure 1.1   An Internet screen

In this figure I have provided a generic screen design. I have indicated several elements of a screen:

- ➡ the standard Internet navigation at the top for the browser you are using;
- ➡ the information in the centre;
- ➡ some words have been underlined;
- ➡ the possibility of other navigational tools at the bottom of the screen.

The words that are underlined indicate that there is more information available at that point. If the learner clicks on an underlined word or phrase, further information is revealed in a set of screens. On the Internet these would be the links to further information about those topics or concepts or tasks available to the learner.

As indicated in the screen, you will need to identify the outcomes for the learners. This means that you will need to identify all the elements of information in the course and provide your learners with attributes to facilitate the development of navigation of your course materials. You should discuss this with the person putting your course on the Internet. This may be you. If so, discuss the linkages with other teachers or a 'critical friend'. This need not be a teacher or learner: their role is to test the logic of the navigation links you have made.

The need for navigation is to make sure the course information is available in a form other than a scrolling text. This allows learners to access the material from multiple viewpoints and covers various learning styles. As the sophistication of your design develops, it should also increase the entry points of learners to the material. This will improve the flexible delivery options of the material.

From the example above, a few of the information screens and possible contents that can be generated from the three underlined terms in Figure 1.2 appear in the screen dumps that follow (Figures 1.3–1.5).

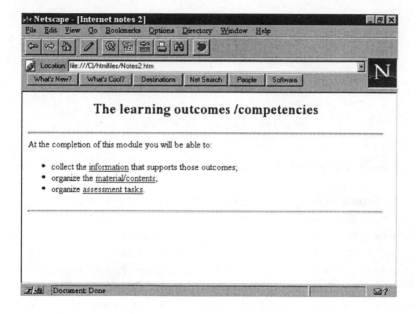

Figure 1.2 A statement of the learning outcomes for an Internet course

From the page shown in Figure 1.2 the student is able to navigate to topics on information, contents or assessments. This page serves as a menu. If the student were to click on the underlined word 'information' they would be presented with a further screen.

As this is only a summary and an indication of the stages I have not identified all the possible links to needed information. However, at the level indicated in Figure 1.3 there is embedded information, eg, on text and video. If you have organized the material properly the learners should be able to access this information from within this page. In other words electronic page-turning or scrolling is at a minimum.

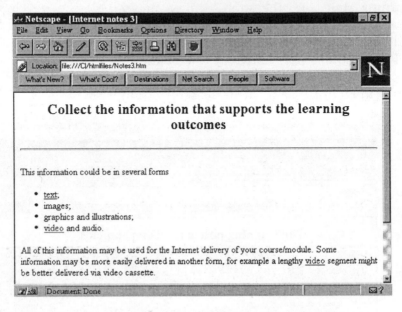

Figure 1.3   Navigation within core information

If the learner had selected the underlined word 'contents', then a screen similar to Figure 1.4(a) would appear. Again it has pointers or links to further information. These could be the assessment tasks as indicated in Figure 1.2. The importance of this is that some learners may be able accelerate their progress if they recognize that this is material they already know.

A drawback of too much text to a page is also illustrated here. In Figure 1.4 all of the information cannot be displayed on the screen at one time. This means that the learner must scroll down the page. Frequently it is the case that scrolling exposes very little extra infor-mation, as Figure 1.4(b) shows. This can be a cause of frustration for the learners. If you had selected security or text or video you would have received pages such as Figures 1.6–1.8.

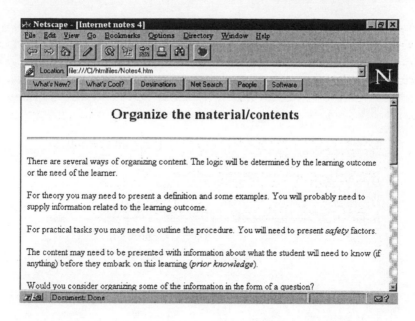

Figure 1.4(a) Considerations about organization

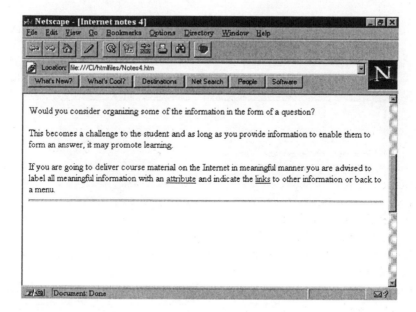

Figure 1.4(b) Scrolling down the screen

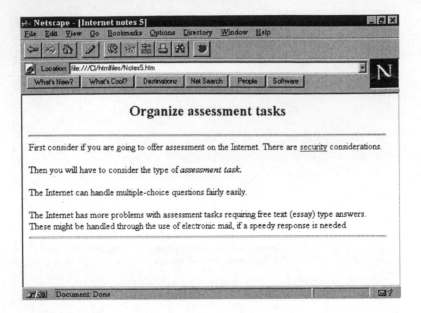

Figure 1.5   Organizing assessment

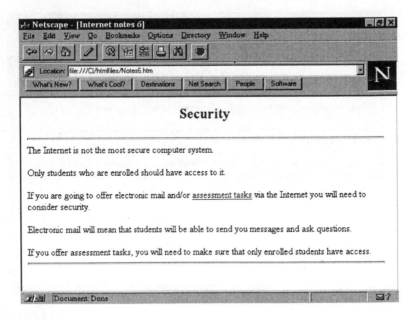

Figure 1.6   Security

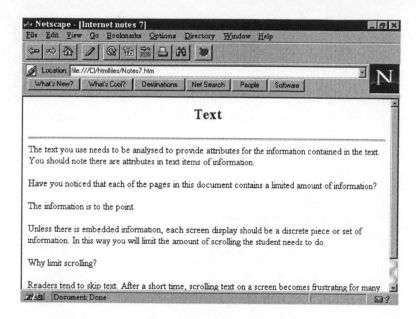

Figure 1.7   Handling of text

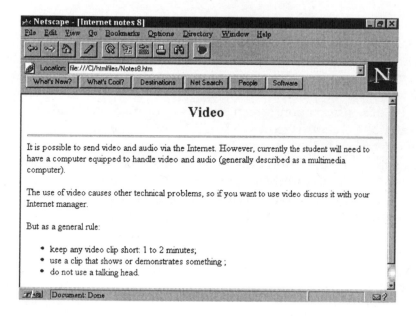

Figure 1.8   Some information about video

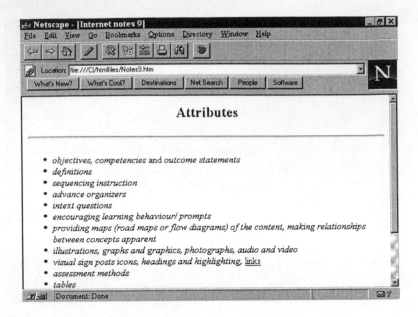

Figure 1.9   A veritable menu of attributes

If these attributes were underlined, they would lead to further information on the attribute. With this amount of information I consider most of it to be at a definition level and I would have the result of a key click or mouse click as a pop-up type display such as Figure 1.10 if you clicked on 'links'.

In this information screen the need to give attributes to course material elements is explained in relation to the development of the presentation on the Internet. If the learner has not come across attributes in their navigation of the course materials then the underlined word 'link' will lead them (point them) to the information available by accessing a screen such as that exampled in Figure 1.9 above. There is at least one other way and that is to negotiate with learners or organizations so that they are not faced with the bewildering array of attributes in Figure 1.9. This process also utilizes the interactive nature of the Internet and treats education and training as a communication process.

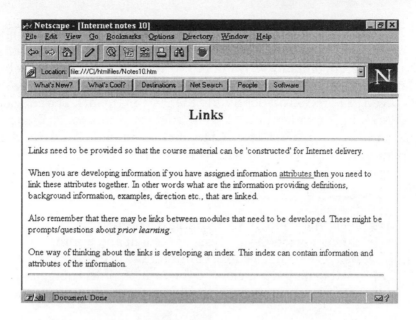

Figure 1.10 Crosslinks

The eclectic/generic approach to Internet course delivery

This approach requires an adoption of the implications in the education and training reform, open and flexible delivery, Just-in-Time education and training and work-related learning. In these settings the need for a formal course may not be required. What may be needed is a set of materials to satisfy the need for a small number of competencies to be addressed, drawn from different subjects.

For example, a company or an individual (note: not an industry) might need to retrain staff or upgrade their skills because of a technological change within the company. In this situation they will require a course suited to their needs, not a course based on industry norms. While an industry-based course in the long term might satisfy the need, it may not address the immediate knowledge and skill requirement. The response of the education or training provider should address the immediate need and this could be through an eclectic or generic approach.

The eclectic or generic approach would have the learner or client company, and the subject expert and an instructional designer, look at the learner or company educational or training need and develop a plan of action. This would have the learner or the client organization involved in a process of identifying their requirements. The education and training organization is then in a position to evaluate the learner–client needs in terms of support material so the desired outcomes will be achieved. The learner or company also now becomes an active learner. They have become an active part of the learning process through:

➡ their involvement in defining the need;
➡ taking part in the analysis of content and appropriate delivery strategies to account for the learners;
➡ establishing the means of verification of learning; and
➡ being part of the evaluation process to verify that needs have been met.

In this scenario the Internet could be a tool for delivery of all or part of the agreed education and training. The Internet may still be an initial contact point but it becomes a means of communication about education and training, not a repository of established courses. There are, however, the possibilities of some generic educational and training materials such as Occupational Health and Safety. These materials could exist in a generic form to be 'fine tuned' for the specific requirements of eclectic requests for materials ranging from childcare to spray-painting.

An organization willing to respond to this learner-centred learning would have a different approach to the design of their home page and subsequent interactive pages. While the shell character of the browser would remain, the core would change from that in Figure 1.1 at the start of this summary (p.2) to the eclectic model in Figure 1.11.

The structured model needs to be compared with a learner-centred model of making the course material available.

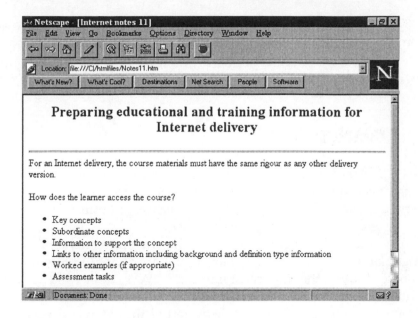

Figure 1.11   An Internet screen for eclectic/generic
course home pages

If the designers of this type of home page are considering the learner, then an option is to download an enquiry file (similar to a computer-based training file) so the learner (organization) is able to work through expressing their need and developing some options offline. When the learner has worked through these options, the file is retransmitted to the institution. Because the file is in the form of a pro-forma, most of the retransmitted information should be able to be handled electronically. It will be the learners' (organizations') variations that will need to be handled on an individual basis. In many cases these variations will be minor.

For example, First Aid Theory for Fishing Operatives, Fire-fighters and Farmers will contain a core element of first aid theory. To make this generic material relevant, it needs to be placed in a setting that is familiar to the learners or will point to common danger areas in their particular occupation. There will be a common element of using machinery but for the fisher folk the first aid incidents will be based on their trade such as cuts, fire and drowning. Firefighters will need to deal with trauma ranging from road accidents to smoke and burns injuries. While it is expected that Farmers will have to deal with injury caused by equipment, it is not beyond the realm of possibility that they will have to cope with fire and drowning. With the ability to navigate, the eclectic learner should be able to find what they want and negotiate an outcome.

Conclusion

This summary is a point of departure, to enable you to start thinking about the development of a course for delivery on the Internet. I emphasize that the ultimate success or failure will link back to the effort put in at the planning stage.

This summary indicates some of the ways of considering course material. It is only after considering the appropriate presentation of course material that the use of Internet (WWW) devices such as icons and graphics in page layout should be considered. Icons bring with them their own problems, while currently the extensive use of complex graphics could be counter-productive. It also reflects that the aim of this book is to consider educational and training issues, while the development of the site, how it will look, will be a product of the design process at the time of the construction of your site.

chapter 2 Why Use the Internet for Teaching and Learning Materials?

There is a great deal of hype about the Internet and the ability of this service to open up access to information for all. One view of the Internet is that it is the alternative method of delivering existing course material. If this is your view then perhaps this book is not for you... or maybe it is. The Internet does offer possibilities to support alternative learning settings, but I am sceptical about much of the current use of the Internet as a means of providing education and training. My main reservation is that an examination of the material on the Internet as an alternative means of the delivery of educational and training material does not live up to the hype. In reality most of the material on the Internet is electronic page-turning at the worst, or an electronic book with some of the random access search facilities and index attributes of a book. Often a so-called educational and training site is pre-book technology. The information is available and presented in the form of a scroll, where you click on the mouse at the down or up arrow to 'scroll' through the content.

Having taken issue with some forms of the presentation of teaching and learning materials on the Internet, there is no denying that it does allow access to information. At the same time, the use of the Internet as an educational and training tool raises questions about how the learning and training are to be sanctioned from this access, particularly if no formal recognition systems are built into the information accessed. New recognition systems of vocational qualifications and key competencies are being established in education and training organizations around the world. It would seem that these education and training organizations are making little use of the Internet. Yet the

Internet offers an interactive setting to satisfy many of the resource demands that the new recognition systems require, particularly in the areas of documenting prior learning and establishing skills gained through informal learning.

The Internet offers the potential to satisfy learners' demands for access to the information they need. Currently, that access is governed by the learners' search skills and the willingness of site-providers to open up access to the computer-based materials they hold,

This book presents the ways in which the Internet can be used to support alternative modes of the delivery of education and training and the traditional face-to-face teaching and learning. The book is written in full knowledge of the fact that educational and training institutions are already offering 'courses' on the Internet. It is also written in the full understanding that most of these offerings are a 'knee-jerk reaction' or an 'increasing the institution profile' exercise. In other words, most of the courses are not purpose-designed. In both cases the effect is that courses are retrofitted to the technology.

Face-to-face teaching and learning, alternative modes of delivery and the Internet

If the Internet is a means of accessing information then it should be a tool for teachers and learners. The use of the Internet changes both the role of the teacher and the role of the learner. If the Internet is a source of information for the course, then this is a significant change in the role of the teacher who in a face-to-face course delivery has been the source of knowledge. With the Internet as a source, the role of the teacher changes. It does not change their expertise, it changes the way they operate and the skills they need. The use of the Internet as a tool in face-to-face teaching turns the delivery into a more flexible educational and training setting and this becomes an alternative mode of delivery. An alternative mode of delivery includes and is the source of open, distance, flexible, mixed mode, peer and mentoring, on and off campus learning, and will need to account for the recognition of prior learning and credit transfer. However, any of these forms of alternative delivery contains within them the notion of central control and the sanctioning of education and training with quality assurance and certification. There is a more subtle and telling implication to alternative methods of delivery.

Alternative methods of delivery address the changing paradigm of education and training. If we are prepared to take a good look at education and training, the process of formal education (school, college, university) works for some. It is hit and miss for others and fails to have a significant impact on the lives of many more. At best, formal education could be described as a haptic activity housed in a rigid time-serving framework established for administrative convenience rather than an outcome for the learner.

This is also a challenge to the intellect and the transition from the old paradigm of 'teaching as telling' and education and training for a lifelong job to the new paradigm of lifelong learning. Freire discusses this stage of transition:

> **"**If men are unable to perceive critically the themes of their time, and thus to intervene actively in reality, they are carried along in the wake of change... Lacking... a critical spirit... man cannot perceive the marked contradictions which occur in society as emerging values in search of an affirmation and fulfilment clash with earlier values seeking self-preservation... This shock between a *yesterday* which is losing relevance but still seeking to survive, and a *tomorrow* which is gaining substance characterizes the phase of transition as a time of announcement and a time of decision. Only, however, to the degree that the choices result from a critical perception of the contradictions are they real and capable of being transformed in action. Choice is illusory to the degree it represents the expectations of others.**"**
>
> (Freire, 1973, p.7. The italics are in the original.)

Without a critical spirit the potential of people to participate in change and determine their future it is limited to the options offered. They do not have the potential or the chance to contribute or to be proactive in the process of change.

In the literature on education and training there is talk of a paradigm shift. This shift is from the expectation that education provides the basis for a job, to an emphasis on education and training as a lifelong process. This shift means that the process of education which could be described as teachers telling is (or must) change to a process of teachers facilitating access to information for the learner. This shift places a greater emphasis on the learner, who is expected to take control of their learning. This is a shift for education from an ordered or imposed process on the learner to a more eclectic activity by the learner. This learner-centred learning also places delivery of the learning materials as a shared responsibility of the learner and the course deliverer. It is in this setting that the Internet has a role to play. But there are assumptions that need to be examined.

With the advent of the wider availability of the Internet there emerges a belief that there is another structure to support teaching and learning. Historically, the development of the Internet was intended for an exchange between peers in the scientific and military community. As such academics are allowed access and an unintended extension is added to an information system. The Internet is seen as a means of the delivery of information and there is an assumption that becomes 'reality': the Internet also has possibilities to assist learning. After all, an exchange of information between peers is an educational process. However, in a teaching and learning situation the exchange is between teachers and learners. This is not an exchange between equals. The development of course materials for the Internet needs to take this imbalance into account.

Then there is the content of the Internet. It is easy to see the sum of human knowledge as an amorphous mass. Historically, to make sense of that mass of information a group of people evolved called subject experts and teachers with the task of making sense of information to others. To do so they compartmentalized and packaged. They selected and edited. They gave structure to parts of the amorphous whole. In doing so, parts were ignored, edited out, disregarded.

While this structuring was going on, the amorphous mass was growing. Illustrative terms such as the 'knowledge explosion' were coined to dramatize this growth. The question then arises of how the subject experts and teachers keep up with the explosion: the answer is that they do not. On the basis of print-based technology and parcel-post delivery, most journal articles are at least twelve months old by the time they reach the reader. This time span includes the conceptualization of the article, writing, the production of the journal and distribution. Computer-based publications through desktop publishing speed up the process. But they still involve an imposed and edited view of the information transmitted. This leads to a final challenge offered to the structure of the old age. This is the challenge to the formal institution of education and training.

Apart from providing economies of scale and time, what purpose is served by the provision of a structure or institution such as an education system? If it is to provide a common heritage then clearly this can arise through random access to the amorphous mass, as easily as by any structured process.

Learning is not entirely learner centred: there are other stakeholders. As Bruner (1990) points out, the 'child enters life as a public process' (p.13). The learning of meaning is developed against a cultural background and as it develops that meaning is shared. The process is public. However, the child is then organized and placed in school to be taught. There may be socio-economic and political reasons for this. However, the process of schooling becomes private: it is conducted behind closed doors between two groups to the virtual exclusion of the public. This process has been challenged in the past in the deschooling movement and in claims that schools decontextualize learning.

Now with the tool of technology such as the Internet and access to the amorphous mass stored on databases, it is possible to be eclectic and build schemata of knowledge that do not conform to an expert or teacher's view of the world. The test of such schemata, if tests are required, will be the learner's ability to use their schema in the world from which they have developed it. The test becomes relevant to the learner, not a reflection of the teacher. The test is also in the public domain, with the outcomes verified through comparison with public access information.

This new paradigm places learning with the learner. It removes the need for gatekeepers or to time-serve or to conform to structures of knowledge built on premises that could be out of date. It has been argued that teachers' failure to use technology is caused by a lack of training, funding shortfalls. However, the real failure of teachers to embrace technology is that technology threatens the primacy of the teacher as a source of knowledge. The old paradigm was that teachers must use the technology to teach the technology. The new paradigm of eclectic education involves learners using technology to learn.

At the same time, little is offered about the Internet having attributes that could hinder learning. There are limitations caused by access and equity issues. These relate to access to the technology, the ability to be supported in that access and limitations caused by the computer-based nature of the Internet.

One limitation of the Internet is the increasing amount of computer technology that is required. The amount of computer memory and the speed of the modems to increase access time are all related to your budget. Although the cost of computer power has dropped, the reality is that most of the possible learners will not have access to this computer power for some time. So you need to be realistic about your delivery.

When the relationship of teaching and learning to aspects of the technology that is represented in the Internet are taken into account, then the Internet is another means of the delivery of teaching and learning material. The set of possibilities need to be taken into account if a course is to be delivered with optimal effect for learners accessing a course on the Internet. Within the spirit of the Internet there is a real potential for an alternative method of delivery to enable the learner to control their learning.

What use are the alternative delivery methods?

Unless a teacher or learner is in an external studies situation, what is the incentive to use alternative methods of delivery in a face-to-face delivery setting?

If the standard delivery setting is face-to-face teaching, determining the delivery methods usually lies with the person delivering the material: the teacher. There are cases in face-to-face teaching of teachers using electronic conferences and electronic messaging systems. Here, the teacher is in charge or initiated the alternative. In most face-to-face teaching, experience shows that teachers will choose a mode of delivery called 'teaching as telling'. The reason is simple. In most cases the delivery of content in a face-to-face setting is the reserve of the subject expert: the teacher. They are also the arbiters of subject content, the presenter of the syntagmatic relationship of information elements within that content and the determiner of the structure and form of delivery.

But, most importantly, the subject expert/teacher will sanction or certify the transition of learners from a naive state to a state that has a certain level of expertise. For many people who teach, the paradigm of 'teaching as telling' is straightforward. It is such a simple exercise to tell, and then test the learner in some way to determine if the person who was told actually learned the information. As such the notion of 'teaching as telling' is very strong.

Instructional design in a traditional setting and alternative delivery

In a formal, structured face-to-face delivery of a course there is an assumption by the teacher and the learner that on successful completion of the course requirements the learner will be deemed to have passed. In many cases the instructional design in face-to-face teaching is a result of teachers translating the requirements of a course outline or syllabus. While the teacher would claim that this translation is a result of analysis, it is also eclectic in that it is a response to a felt need or feedback from learners as their response in a real-time event.

However, in the delivery of a course in any non-traditional setting (that is, not face-to-face) the instructional design will be a result of consultation involving subject experts and the designers of instruction. These consultations will be about the use of teaching and learning strategies to encourage the learning process. These consultations need to be made public to counter the strong possibility that questions and concerns will be raised by those entrenched in formal education about the learners' abilities using non-traditional education and training delivery. Not the least of these questions will be how to verify the learning that takes place when it is not conducted in a sanctioned environment or a supervised place. In part, this is the dilemma that faces all teachers and learners who have worked through correspondence courses. It faces all learners seeking certification of their prior learning and experience.

In the face-to-face setting there is a question about why any teacher would complicate matters by using alternative methods in their course. But is that the same as saying why use methods other than 'teaching as telling' if these methods and associated technologies are appropriate? One possible answer may be that alternative delivery methods are seen by subject experts and teachers as having nothing to do with the needs of learners or with the learners' requirements for one or more aspects of open, distance, flexible, mixed-mode, peer and mentoring, on and off campus, the recognition of prior learning, credit transfer, quality assurance and certification. Another possible answer is that these means of delivery challenge teachers. These means of delivery may also place the content in a public domain and possibly out of the control of teachers.

At the same time these alternative methods of delivery may be novel to those brought up in traditional academic life in the hallowed halls, ivy walls and musty library stalls. However, there is a long tradition of many of these methods of delivery of education. It would be an insult to institutions such as the School of the Air in Australia and the effective correspondence schools around the world to pretend that many of the methods they use are alternative and by inference that they are second-rate or soft options. In reality the use of the Internet is another communication tool. As a delivery tool for education and training it is no more than a technological enhancement of delivery methodologies that these distance education organizations pioneered.

This process of teaching has been written about extensively. Most of this writing urges the practitioner to have a curriculum document that is sanctioned by the appropriate authorities, a sound set of objectives and learning materials for the students to use with a valid set of assessment tools. The assumption underlying this is that teaching is about content. In many areas of the curriculum that assumption may still be true. But there is increasing evidence of the need to teach or to foster the ability of the student to become an independent lifelong learner. This trend has implications for the role of lecturers and the process of teaching.

Davies after Gagné (1987) wrote about the nine events of instruction. His taxonomy starts with events in the classroom and the actions that could be taken to promote learning during a lesson. Gagné and Briggs (1974) outlined a process of instructional design. Romiszowski (1988, 1989) deliberates on instructional methodologies. Merrill (1991, 1993) is concerned with instructional transactions. In his writing, instructional transactions are seen as 'patterns of learner interactions... which have been designed to enable a learner to acquire a certain kind of knowledge' (1991, p.2).

Laurillard (1987) describes instruction as being didactic and/or communication-based. The difficulty is that all these descriptions and theories deal with classroom activities derived from course documents, as if the translation from course document to classroom or teaching was a seamless process. The limitation arises because all to often a formula or stereotypical response is used from the strategies and resources that are known, not from the full range of possibilities.

An intervening strategy is about to be suggested that not only addresses this limitation but also suggests a means of fostering the ability to initiate and innovate in education and training.

The theoretical considerations of Davies, Gagné and Briggs, Romiszowski and their peers need careful consideration because they alert the practitioner to details that need to be borne in mind in teaching practice. What is being suggested here is that there is a superordinate set of four instructional modes that need to be considered alongside a course document and prior to considerations of teaching strategies.

In considering these four modes, the final outcome is for learners to learn. This is what the methodologies of Davies, Gagné and peers are directed towards. However, it remains a vexed question made all the more problematic because no matter what is done in the name of teaching, during the course of teaching, different students seem to 'learn' differently.

The superordinate modes

An examination of course documents reveals implied modes of discourse. These modes could be considered under the four headings of didactic, illustrative, vicarious and experiential.

Didactic

In this mode, an analysis of the course document will determine what required knowledge is a series of 'knowns'. As such, the appropriate type of classroom activities may be developed.

Illustrative

An analysis of course documents for illustrative requirements will determine course content needs for material and activities to familiarize the learner with activities and processes to enrich their knowledge and provide examples beyond a 'case of one'.

Vicarious

An analysis of course documentation may determine the need for vicarious experiences. In this situation the learner is asked to play a role as part of an activity. The purpose of vicarious modes is to familiarize the participant in an activity that closely resembles the real world. In this setting the student is able to 'control' the situation and learn from mistakes without paying the price of real mistakes. The vicarious experience is particularly suited to hazardous and difficult situations in preparation for the real experience.

Experiential

The analysis of course documentation may determine the need for experiential processes. In this situation the student is working through a real-life situation. The student may well be working on a project, perhaps even a model, but the project is based on a real-world event. In all cases the results of the student's actions have a real outcome. The intention of the experiential mode is for the student to demonstrate the transfer of theoretical knowledge to practical skills.

Implications for teaching and learning

First, the proposal for superordinate considerations in the translation from course document to teaching and learning does nothing to affect the course documentation undertaken in teaching. It may have some implications for reorienting a focus on to the work of learners.

In the first instance, these modes are applied to the course document, not to the classroom activities. Second and most importantly the suggested activities go beyond those normally or stereotypically associated with the names: teaching, example, exercise and practical. The use of the mode analysis of course documents is to break out of the usual as a response. The use of mode analysis is based on the following considerations:

> ➡ there is more to the process of teaching than standing in front of a class and telling;

➡ there is more to examples than the mere setting and providing of answers;

➡ there is more to exercises than doing the activity;

➡ finally, there is more to a practical activity than its completion.

A further implication of the use of mode analysis is that it does nothing to alter a teaching style in terms of preparation, planning and presentation. Teaching will still require introduction, exposition, reiteration, feedback and evaluation. Teaching will still require remediation and testing. However, the use of mode analysis may require the scope for teaching and learning activities to be broadened.

Another implication will be in the expectation placed on students. They will have to be active in their learning process. 'Teaching as telling' has the students being passive. A change towards or an increase in illustrative and vicarious experiences requires the students to become more active participants in the learning process. This increase in activity on the students' part should not be seen as lecturers doing less. In fact, lecturers will be just as important to the learning process, but activities such as the guidance of student work will become more central to the lecturer's role than the 'teaching' function. Students will still learn, but lecturers will become 'coordinators of learning experiences' (Rogers, 1969).

The use of mode analysis could cause concerns about change in an already full curriculum and teaching process. This can be countered with the argument that the sign of a mature organization is that it recognizes material and content that can be discarded, or at least treated with reduced emphasis. In skills training there may be some argument for retaining simpler, less expensive equipment for teaching the basics before progressing to 'state-of-the-art' equipment. On the other hand, if the industry is state-of-the-art, it is correct to ask what use is old technology? The argument is similar to the one that possibly still rages in some quarters on the use by students of calculators with function keys.

Implications for learning

If these four modes are seen as a superordinate set of organizational tools for the teaching and learning process, the task then becomes one of identifying the modes of learning best suited to the course itself.

More importantly, the decisions about whether part of a course is didactic, illustrative, vicarious or experiential places a focus on the learner. This in turn focuses on aspects such as the learner's prior knowledge and experience. In doing so, questions arise about the methods used to proceed with decisions about the treatment of the course content. In reality the questions that arise will place an emphasis on the presentation which has teaching being more than standing in front of a class and telling, which uses examples that are more than setting and providing answers, which has exercises that are more than doing the activity, and experiential activity which involves more than mere completion.

Conclusion

This is a practical scheme to consider and incorporate the diversity of education and training possibilities when translating course documents to course delivery materials and activities. The use of superordinate modes or organizers can potentially break down stereotypical decision-making at the crucial stage of translation from course documentation to the course material that is offered to the students. The use of superordinate modes or organizers expands traditional teaching and learning beyond traditional teaching functions and is based on the assumption that people are no longer trained for a job; they are to be educated or trained for lifelong learning to maintain their skills and employability.

What is the Internet (for education and training)?

In its simplest form, the Internet is an electronic mail system and library access facility. It is a mail system because it allows you to send messages. The messaging capabilities of the Internet should allow you to make enquiries, enrol and communicate with a teacher, download information and complete course tasks. You should also be able to communicate with peers who are completing the same course and be informed of your progress through the course. It is a library access system because it allows requests for information. But, like any library system, you need to know what you are looking for. In an educational and training setting the library capabilities of the Internet should allow you to browse for the course or information you seek. This use of electronic communication raises a set of issues relating to a paradigm shift.

What use are the alternative delivery methods?

The world is becoming choked by a new set of highways and infrastructures. Most of them are electronic. However, as with the physical highways, these electronic highways have an ironic example such as the paperless office. There is emerging evidence that many institutions are facing some of these issues by limiting access to printers and photocopies so they achieve paperless office status and reduce the costs of operation.

However, as part of the paradigm shift from teacher-centred learning to lifelong learning, there is a need to change the way we think about education and training in the information age. Rather than alternative delivery with the implication that the learner is sent information from a central resource controlled by a teacher or institution, we should be thinking of the use of communication tools such as the Internet as a means of allowing the learner to access course content. To place the current communications methods and see them in an alternative delivery there is a need to retrace a few steps in the development of this information age.

The first step towards the electronic information process was the development of databases. These databases allowed the storage of information within a structured framework. The framework was designed for easy retrieval by anyone with the authority to access the database. In the early days of databases, there were genuine concerns that the integrity of the database could be corrupted. However, some organizations soon recognized that the information could provide commercial advantage when made available to appropriate sections, subsidiaries and, in some cases, sales staff and representatives. It became obvious that without corrupting the database it was possible to provide up-to-date information from the database to various parts of the organization. This resulted in the development of distributed databases with access on a 'need to know' basis. With sanctioned authority, certain people have a right to know. And this right was attributed to people to do their particular job: they had no understanding of or need to understand the larger structure of the data they were accessing.

Then there was the second step towards an electronic information process. This happened when an organization realized the need for the 'corporate' information to be known at several levels within the organization. It meant that a previously fundamental aspect of the management of knowledge was replaced: It was no longer the prerogative of a high official to dispense it. Suddenly the need for access to data and to provide data came from below.

In the corporate world there is a third step. This is when the available information is used as teaching and learning material. In many organizations there is an increasing tendency to use real corporate information. In a corporate setting it makes sense, and as long as security is tightly in place, the use of corporate information, imagining the status of the organization places the learner close to the real world.

In the education and training setting the placing of subject expertise into information banks (databases) available to all has implications for the institution and is not a true comparison with an internal education and training enterprise within a corporation. Yet the communications options are open and there is a possibility that educational and training institutions may be able to benefit from the availability of the Internet as a tool. However, any educational and training organization will need to be clear in their intent.

The future in the short term

In discussing alternative delivery and the reception of information, the existence of databases, the development of global networks, such as the Internet, and the development of conglomerates of news and entertainment (and/or edutainment) companies, it is not too difficult to predict the outcome over the next two years. It is possible to predict that in certain areas of education and training the following will or has happened. In the USA 'Super Mario Brothers' will take over the major teaching role in maths and science within the cable networks. 'Carmen Maranda' has already done that for the geography of places on the computer. Similarly, programmes from the 'Sesame Street' stable exist for languages at elementary level, while the Grolier Encyclopaedia CD-ROM provides answers to all in grade school assignments. These alternative modes of delivery still see 'teaching as telling' as the main information-transfer (teaching and learning) technique. Although a comprehensive range of subjects may not be currently available, what will become available through cable, Internet or satellite delivery into the home will be a version of formal, sanctioned education. Home and workplace access to education has (or will have) a similar legal status as school/college/university-based education.

In this scenario, the alternative methods of delivery are those the learner has access to and can use. The learner has access to the knowledge base (the sum total of human knowledge). The instruction may take place with or without expert guidance: it is also of little matter. The learner has access to experience that is real, or through simulation, or through virtual reality. The learner has access to the means of testing their skills and knowledge. One result is that alternative methods of delivery and access are available to those who have access to technology, so it will be the affluent who are able to afford alternative delivery or access.

A different way of thinking about alternative methods of delivery is to decide that the delivery be technology neutral. This is not to deny the use of technology but to make sure it is not a reason why potential learners are denied or unable to access course material. Any course developed with alternative delivery means must have options that ensure that all learners study a course with the same rigour, challenges and outcomes, irrespective of the method of course delivery. So it is important to compare the aspects of a fully functional Internet with options such as two-way video and voice, still images, graphics, text with e-mail and text and audio-based conferencing as other methods or options for alternative delivery. One of the main characteristics to be considered is the potential for interaction. The ability to interact is a key feature of face-to-face teaching. It is therefore important to decide what actual or equivalent levels of interaction are possible in other forms of delivery and access.

The importance of interaction

Interaction is one of the higher order levels of feedback that behaviourists and cognitivists agree are important in the educational process (Mory, 1992). Those who see education as a construct would also include feedback and more importantly interaction as a needed feature in education (Bruner, 1990; Laurillard, 1993).

In the face-to-face mode of course delivery it is an assumption that learners learn through a combination of interaction with the learning materials and their teachers. How a learner learns is a product of a combination of factors that include the learner's maturity, the learning materials, the teacher and other factors such as the support the learner is getting for their learning endeavours.

If we look at a range of delivery options, the ability of the learner to interact with material and teacher varies. For example, even in the face-to-face mode of teaching the availability of interaction ranges from a one-on-one consultation between the teacher and the learner, a one-to-many interaction between a teacher or tutor and a class or tutorial group, to the questionable interaction between a lecturer in a lecture hall and the 100+ learners in the hall.

Underlying the delivery question and the potential to interact is the economy of scale that might be involved. It is obvious that a one-on-one interaction between a learner and a teacher is possibly more expensive than a one-to-many tutorial where the answers by the tutor/teacher or the enquiries of the learners can be shared among the larger audience of the class/tutorial.

In Figure 2.1, the vertical lefthand column lists different methods of education and training. The headings on the horizontal axis are indicators of the type of audio-visual material for the methodology, the potential distribution area, the currently available technology to serve these needs alongside a notional comparison of cost. The final column indicates the resulting uses. These are not the only uses of the method of education and training, but the most likely uses given the expertise of teachers. Figure 2.1 is my development based on a chart by Schamber (1988).

Figure 2.1   Chart of media characteristics

Methods of education and training	Type of images and sound	Distribution range	Technology	Delivery cost on a notional comparison	Resulting type of use
Face-to-face	As selected by the teacher	The class or lecture*	As selected by the teacher	With capital costs written off recurrent costs	Generally 'teaching as telling' except as dictated by content needs such as experiments
Correspond-ence	Print, audio and video tape	By post*	As selected by the teacher	Postal costs	Generally 'teaching as telling' but some interaction through mail or phone
Audio-graphics	Text, stills and sound. There is also a slow scan video option	Depends on telephone network Internet	Proprietary brands	Not expensive to purchase or use	Sharing images and discussion. Interactive two-way vision and sound
Computer files	Text, images and possible motion through video capture	Depends on computer network LAN WAN e-mail Internet	Need not be limited to a single operating system	Not expensive to purchase or use	Collaboration: the use of shared documents and actions. Interactive two-way transfer of information
Video tape	Motion and sound. Quality of video depends on production equipment	Distribution by mail. Possible via Internet	Ranges from expensive studio to inexpensive camcorders	Ranges according to equipment. The distribution is the cost of mailing	Demonstrations. showing examples. Passive but generates interest
Closed circuit	Motion and sound	Limited to the network or LAN, WAN and Internet	Middle of the road	Minimal after establishing the network	Demonstration showing examples. May be interactive
ISDN 128 Kbyte Video conference Cable	Motion and sound. Not broadcast quality video	Limited to the network possible Internet	More costly than closed circuit	Minimal after establishing the network. Cost of call plus a premium in some areas	Full two-way vision and sound. Demonstrations discussions collaboration

Methods of education and training	Type of images and sound	Distribution range	Technology	Delivery cost on a notional comparison	Resulting type of use
Cable	Motion and sound. Quality of video depends on production equipment	Limited to the network equipment ISDN nodes possible Internet	Not too costly. Main expense is the encoder and video compression equipment	Minimal after establishing the network	Showing examples. May be interactive with the use of keypads or telephone
Microwave	Motion and sound	Limited to range of dish or network of dishes and any repeater stations.‡	Costly. Dishes, site location costs, line hire from distribution centre to dish	Minimal after establishing the network of Dishes and repeated stations costs of transmission	Demonstration showing examples. May be interactive with the use of a telephone
Instructional fixed service (IFTS in USA)	Motion and sound	Limited to broadcast service strength usually 25 miles ‡	Costly. Transmitter and line cost	Minimal after establishing the transmitter. Costs of transmission	Demonstration showing examples. May be interactive with the use of a telephone
Broadcast TV	Motion and sound	Limited to broadcast range ‡	Costly. Studio transmitter	Costly	One-way vision and sound. Audio only. Interaction through telephone (generally)
Satellite	Motion and sound	Limited to footprint ‡	Costly. Production facilities	Costly transponder hire. Uplink lease downlink site	One-way vision and sound. Audio only. Interaction through telephone (generally)

*   potential for Internet on campus. If there is a phone line and modem and computer, Internet can follow.
‡   capable of carrying Internet information.

As Figure 2.1 indicates there are many ways of distributing course material. These delivery tools, such as broadcast television, video cassette and video-conferencing support the use of the Internet. At the same time, the Internet incorporates many existing features of class-room presentation.

Figure 2.1 also indicates that the delivery mechanisms have 'inbuilt' interaction. That is, there are 'real-time' features incorporating inter-action as part of the technology, such as audio graphics, computer file-sharing and video-conferencing. Of these three, only ISDN video-conferencing (and proprietary brand-based video-conference equipment) and the developments in computer technology allow for 'full' motion video and audio 'both ways'. The Internet is a technology that can use these interactive features.

The possibilities of using the Internet seem encouraging. However, the reality is that there is the potential to repeat all the mistakes of the implementation of other electronic media and we will end up with electronic page-turning, limited or no interaction and the inability for the teacher and learner to interact in real-time or even communicate. So there is a need to recognize the changing roles of teachers and learners in education and training.

Changing role of the teacher

With the advent of course material on the Internet the role of the teacher must change. Gone is the need for the teacher to be the source of all knowledge. The required knowledge for the course is in the Internet delivery materials. However, there is still a role for the teacher that relates to the knowledge, skills and attitudes associated with the course. In the absence of a truly intuitive computer-based intelligent system to guide the learner, they will probably need assistance during the course. This is where the changed role of the teacher emerges. Contrary to an expectation that the teacher's role will diminish with the advent of a computer-based course, or an Internet-delivered course, the demands on the teacher's time remain the same and indeed may even increase. However, the types of demand change, and this is where the teacher will have to change their role in order to provide a service to the learners. One of the initial changes is that the teacher becomes a monitor and mentor. The teacher's role becomes less instructional and more supporting. As a mentor, the 'teacher' may need to provide high-level support for the learner. However, as the learner gains confidence, these levels of support can be negotiated down.

Some of the functions that are not usually part of a face-to-face teachers' repertoire and skills that they will need to develop include:

- the use of electronic mail for messages;
- participation in chat and bulletin board sessions;

➡ the use of computer managed learning applications for test generation;

➡ scoring and updating learner records; and

➡ the electronic receipt of free text submissions such as essays and open ended questions.

While the ability to use the technology will facilitate the new skills required by teachers, what is important is the ability of the course developers to make the material into accessible information. If the design of the materials does not support learners' ability to learn and teachers' ability to be mentors and guides, then learners will become frustrated and disillusioned and ultimately drop out of the Internet-delivered course. Inevitably this will result in teachers also becoming anti-Internet.

In the best-case scenario this will not happen: there will be resources to support the appropriate development for materials on the Internet and support for teachers to change their role. This change in their role is mirrored by a changing role for the learner.

Changing role of the learner

With course material on the Internet, the role of the learner changes from one of primarily being a recipient to one of being a participant. If the course materials are designed for optimal interaction, the learner becomes a searcher with a level of responsibility for their learning that is generally not available in face-to-face teaching. Just as the teacher will have to learn new tools, the learners will also have to use new tools if they are to fully capitalize on using course materials and related sources of information available on the Internet. This will include:

➡ search and enquiry design;

➡ ability to download material to work offline;

➡ the use of electronic mail;

➡ the use of file transfer for test and assessment tasks and for communication with class peers and teacher.

Conclusion

The Internet does allow access to information. However, this does not mean that putting course materials (information) on the Internet is effective for the learner. In the face-to-face mode of course delivery it is an assumption that learners learn through a combination of interaction with the learning materials and their teachers. The use of an alternative method of delivery such as the Internet only addresses the reality of education and training when the rigour in the course materials and the possibility for the learners to interact with the teacher are similar to the rigour and interaction in a face-to-face delivery of a course. This position is only supported because face-to-face teaching is seen as the norm.

Yet a real expectation for the use of the Internet in course delivery is that, contrary to an expectation that the role of the teacher will diminish with Internet or computer-based course delivery, the demands on the teachers' time remain the same and may increase. However, the types of demand change. This is where the teacher must change in order to provide a service to the learners. One of the initial changes is that the teacher becomes a monitor and mentor. The teacher's role becomes less instructional and more supportive. At the same time the Internet changes the role of the learner from one of recipient to participant.

chapter **3**   General Considerations

Summary

There are two considerations about using the Internet as a delivery mechanism. The first consideration when placing course material on the Internet is its source. You will need to decide whether you are developing a new course specifically using the Internet as your primary or sole means of delivery.

The second is whether you are developing a version of an existing course to be delivered partly or wholly via the Internet alongside other versions of the course.

The first section of this chapter looks at the characteristics of educational and training courses. The character of the course relates to the amount of theory and practical work involved in it. It is against an examination of the course for theoretical and practical work that it is possible to make some decisions about it and its appropriateness for access using the Internet. After this general examination, the chapter looks at factors affecting the selection of appropriate course content for new courses and for revising existing courses into a format suitable for Internet access. There is an underlying assumption that this analysis will have to satisfy students' needs.

Types of courses

For the purposes of this chapter I am assuming that no subject area is unsuited for delivery through the Internet. This does not mean that some content may be inappropriate for delivery on the Internet. However, the purpose here is to discuss characteristics that make course materials appropriate for Internet delivery. I will consider the characteristics of courses as being on a continuum.

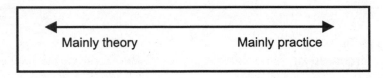

Figure 3.1   Characteristics of a course as a continuum

It is often difficult to classify a course solely as a theory course or as purely a practical course. In reality most theory courses ask the learner to demonstrate their knowledge through some 'practical' test, be it an essay, an exam or some other form of assessment task. A reverse situation arises with practical courses. Most practical courses have a rationale or theory component. The theory may be made explicit through a theory session or the theory may be passed on implicitly as explanations during the demonstration that are needed in practical sessions. If the Internet is to be used, it does have attributes and these need to be considered. The Internet must not be seen as a panacea in the way in which many of the technologies have been promoted. There must be a means of selecting appropriate content based on the strengths and limitations of the Internet.

Selection of appropriate course content for Internet delivery

This is the wrong way to plan and prepare course materials. It is as though you have made up your mind to use the Internet and you will force-fit your materials into an Internet delivery. This really is a case of the technology driving the development. It might be timely for you to do a Strengths, Weaknesses, Opportunities and Threats (SWOT) analysis of using the Internet as a delivery tool before progressing any further. These will be some of the factors you will think about. You may also have specific problems in any of the quadrants which will need to be documented.

Strengths	Weaknesses
➡ Internet a growth area: increases exposure for course offering ➡ Course material already instructionally designed ➡ Industries moving into Internet-capable operations opens up potential for learners to access course material on the job ➡ Use human ability to control and program computers	➡ Currently access to the Internet for some learners ➡ Course material already instructionally designed (but not revised for the Internet) ➡ Reluctance of teachers to use technology ➡ Lack of an Internet standard ➡ Possibility of electronic page-turning if the course material lacks design
Opportunities	**Threats**
➡ Frees up teaching spaces ➡ Opens up enrolment opportunities ➡ Recognition as education and training leader if best practice followed ➡ Reuse existing resources, giving cost benefit	➡ To status as provider if not at the leading edge ➡ To teachers who need to alter their teaching style ➡ To credibility if inappropriate implementation

Figure 3.2   An example of SWOT analysis

On the basis of weighing up the aspects of the SWOT analysis in Figure 3.2 the decision might be that the Internet is a means of delivery of course material. However, it does not give an indication of what type of course is appropriate. Not even consulting the chart in Figure 2.1 (p.29) will indicate the type of course material appropriate for the Internet. Figure 2.1 indicates that the Internet is capable of supporting most course-delivery methods. It might be that the use of the Internet as a delivery tool is capable of supporting course delivery without the need to resort to other technologies, if the course content is appropriate. You will have to determine the resources and delivery tools you need for your course and then argue for their funding.

At this point, and to decide whether the content and the needs of the learners, not the technology is driving the method of delivery, you should refer to Figure 3.3 on the strengths and weaknesses of the Internet as a way of delivering course material. I have used a simplification of theory and practice on the left-hand side to open up consideration of strengths and weaknesses.

If you have been through the analysis in Figures 3.2 and 3.3 and your overwhelming urge to place course materials on the Internet remains, then perhaps the need is driven by the needs of the learners and the course and not the desire by course presenters to be on the Internet. If this is the case then the following sections apply.

New course specifically for the Internet

Here you will have to set about the usual tasks of determining the needs, outcomes for learners and expectations of accreditation. Or do you need to? If you take the current spirit of the Internet and you have information that you think others may be interested in, then perhaps it is a matter of 'publish and be damned'?

However, producing a course for delivery on the Internet is different (even if only slightly) to publishing information. A course has some structure with agreed outcomes. A course has overtones of a contract: certainly enrolment in a course is contractual because the learner has expectations that will be fulfilled through participation in it. If the learner is asked for money and pays, then a contract is formed. So the formal elements of fulfilling a contract are required. This is far beyond a mere enquiry that is a connotation of 'surfing the net'.

Type of course	Strengths of the Internet	Weaknesses of the Internet
Mainly theory	➡ Linking of information sources ➡ Potential for developing metacognition ➡ Handles e-mail type communications ➡ Possibility of chat and bulletin boards for information	➡ Potentially only screen-based information ➡ Lack of defined audit trail ➡ Problems with free text answers
Mainly practice	➡ Potential of computer-like patience in dealing with examples ➡ Possibility of simulations ➡ Drill and practice ➡ Handling of structured assessment tasks ➡ Bulletin boards for information ➡ Possible sequential presentation of examples, worked examples and demonstrations	➡ Various access tools (browsers) mean the fidelity of presentation may not be maintained, eg graphics audio and visuals may not be available to the learner if they have 'different' computers (Blame the technology) This should be a decreasing problem as cross-platform technology arrives
General considerations	**Strengths of the Internet**	**Weaknesses of the Internet**
	➡ Individual and enterprise support ➡ Ability to update course materials ➡ Capable of incorporating: Video Audio Still photos Text Information from other sources/sites	➡ Lack of standards (though *de facto* standards exist) ➡ Who has the skills and who does the updating on Internet material? ➡ How will your site handle the considerable demand on computer capacity required by the file sizes of video, images and audio (even with current compression technology)?

Figure 3.3   Strengths and weaknesses of the Internet as a delivery option

If you are developing a new course for delivery using the Internet as your primary delivery mechanism, you will need to go through the same steps of developing the instructional design for any course. You will need to:

➡ analyse the need for a course and establish the required outcomes;
➡ establish the knowledge, skills and attitudes required to progress learners towards the outcomes;

39

➡ develop a substrata of tasks to ensure that the knowledge, skills and attitudes are addressed; and

➡ develop a valid scheme and set of tasks and tests to make sure that the expected outcomes developed through the initial analysis for the learner are met.

This gives the impression of a 'teacher-dominated' curriculum. But the intention is to make the context apparent to the learner to enable them to negotiate meaningful learning scenarios. While you are going through those steps you will need to remember the attributes of the Internet that you are going to have to work around, and those attributes of the Internet that will enhance your teaching and learning materials.

Developing an existing course for delivery on the Internet

In all respects, any course offered through different methods or means must be offered with the same rigour, challenges and outcomes no matter what forms of delivery are used. A course delivered face-to-face will have the same outcomes as a course offered by correspondence or through variations in the use of media for delivery such as computers or broadcast video or modes of delivery such as off-campus. It is not simply a matter of putting your course material on a computer file, running a mark-up language over the top of it and calling it an Internet-delivered course. At best you will have electronic page-turning or even seemingly endless scrolling, neither of which will endear you to the learner. More importantly, this form of presentation will soon tarnish any possibility for the Internet to be accepted as a valid tool for education and training. So the transformation of a course from one version to an Internet version requires three steps.

The first step is to review the assumptions on which your course was based. You will need to:

➡ make sure the need for the course and the required outcomes are still relevant;

➡ confirm the knowledge skills and attitudes required;

➡ examine the substrata of tasks to ensure that the knowledge skills and attitudes are addressed; and

➡ check that there is a valid scheme and set of tasks and tests to make sure that the expected outcomes are tested and the learner satisfies the criteria/competencies as required.

You will then need to review the course-support material, the teachers notes and class handouts or learners guides to make sure that the information required is available. One of the possible problems you might face is that your teachers materials and the learners guides are in skeletal form. In other words, it is possible to see the structure and the concepts of the course, but there is a lack of content substance. This is understandable. If the course was prepared for face-to-face teaching, then it is the role of the teacher to provide that flesh on the skeleton. At the same time the role of the learner is to transfer the information provided by the teacher to their workbooks.

If there seems to be a lack of information in the course materials, the teacher's notes and the learner's notes, then you are faced with the options of halting the process of using this course (lack of resources) or committing further resources to overcome the shortfall in information. This decision will be made more difficult depending on the length and complexity of the course.

In a short course of six to eighteen hours, many of the points that make up the skeleton may require nothing more than short text passages, annotated illustrations, diagrams and photographs, or the inclusion of short video and audio clips to make the meaning clearer and serve as points of interaction with the learner. In a more substantial course of 300 hours, the task of gathering information to flesh out the skeleton may require considerable resources.

At this decision-making point you will also need to consider assessment tasks and reporting. If this course is being offered by another method, you will need to consider how you are going to make assessment tasks the equivalent of the assessment tasks in the other method of delivery. Two factors are at play here. The first is the perception of learners of being able to pass a course: is this Internet course offering a 'soft' option? The second factor is the form and style of the evaluation task.

A course delivered by the Internet or partly through the Internet falls into the category of alternative delivery. As such, the course is open to questioning by 'traditionalists' who question the authenticity of any course delivery that is not directly under the control of a face-to-face teacher. Two examples of the problem of directly relating face-to-face learner assessment with assessment of learners using an Internet delivered course are now described.

Example one

Common time for undertaking an assessment

In the face-to-face method of delivery, all learners generally undertake an assessment task at the same time. As such, the chance to compare notes only happens after the assessment event. In a course delivered by the Internet, this may not be the case. Learners may reach an assessment task at different times. Given the connections available on the Internet, probably information about assessment tasks (not the actual assessment task) will probably become known through the e-mail and chat sessions that an Internet-delivered course will encourage. This is not so much a security issue as an issue of how to devise assessment tasks for the Internet course so that they remain valid.

Example two

Determining the equivalence between different methods of delivery of a course

In the face-to-face delivery of a course, teachers and learners develop an insight into the way the learners are moving through the course materials as these are presented to them by the teacher. This perspective of the learners' progress is reinforced, or called into question, as the interactions take place between learners and teachers. These perceptions will also be reinforced by the teachers assessment tasks and the learners' ability to respond to the tasks. For the learner on the Internet, the task of interaction is one of proaction. The information and the assessment tasks may be delivered by the Internet – but what of the learners' interaction with the teacher? If the learner is computer literate, then the 'overhead' of using a computer as a means of communication will be minimal. If the learner is not computer literate or unused to the communication protocols of the Internet, there will be some reluctance to communicate. How is the teacher to interpret minimal communication or even none at all?

The Internet and education and training

There is a tension between the concept of the Internet as a source of information and as a tool for education and training. The Internet is seen as a source of information. The enquirer or learner accesses and accumulates sites that contain information. In the absence of any formal course, it is up to the enquirer or learner what they do with this eclectic education. On the other hand, there is an expectation that a learner working through a course delivered via the Internet will be undertaking a sanctioned course and that this course will result in some form of certificate, diploma or degree.

The tension arises for the eclectic learner if later on they need to certify their learning from random accessing of the information. This is possible through recognition of prior learning. However if they have not requested certification at the time of 'study', these eclectic learners will now have to provide evidence of study. The immediate answer to resolving this is an administrative one of paying fees. This, however, denies the current myth that all information on the Internet is free.

Conclusion

In this chapter the characteristics of a course relate to the amount of theory and practical work involved in it. It is against an examination of the course for theoretical and practical work that it is possible to make some decisions about a course and the courses appropriateness for delivery using the Internet. One of the key examinations is to determine a SWOT analysis of the Internet and relating that to the characteristics of the course you want to offer. After this general examination, the chapter looked at factors affecting the selection of appropriate course content for new courses about to be developed and for revising existing courses from another format suitable for Internet delivery. An underlying assumption has been that the rigour of the course being delivered or supported through the use of the Internet is equivalent to any other form of delivery.

chapter 4   Getting Started: The Internet and Instructional Design

Summary

There is little experience in using the Internet as a teaching and learning tool. There is experience and research on computer-based learning. This has given insights to elements of screen design, the development of interaction through online and offline working, file transfers and the evolution of the computer into an audio-visual communication device. It is my hope that through the examination of a SWOT analysis of the Internet and the problems of computer-based learning, when courses are made available through the Internet there will be effective teaching and learning in the material.

At the moment there is very little experience of delivering courses via the Internet. However, there is a field of experience in delivering courses by computer, so one expectation is that the same strengths and weakness that apply to computer-based learning will apply to some aspects of teaching and learning on the Internet.

However, these are not the only considerations. Currently there are available computer-based tools that allow the direct conversion of a word-processed file to be converted to pages on the Internet. These are Hypertext Markup Language (HTML) and Standard Generalized Markup Language (SGML). There is HOT JAVA for graphics, Page Mill and Site Mill for page and site maintenance and a virtual reality modelling language alongside a version of CAD that provides 3D modelling. Microsoft Word has an add-on called Internet Assist. By simply (it is almost simple) converting the file from a text (.doc) file through the 'save as' process, a standard word-processed document is converted into a scrollable HTML text page that could be used on the Internet. However, all that happens is a simple conversion; but more than just a simple conversion is needed to make this material educationally appropriate for use on the Internet. If this is the cheap and easy way you want to 'get a course on the Internet' then there are several textbooks on this conversion process, or discuss it with your local computer experts. The actual process of putting material on the Internet is not that difficult, but without development the material may offer limited teaching and learning outcomes.

If you want to extend the teaching and learning process through the use of the Internet you will need to spend time considering the options. Careful analysis is needed to ensure that the materials that go on the Internet are quality teaching and learning materials, which will promote meaningful teaching and learning activities. This means developing a more sophisticated view of the materials when they are translated from a face-to-face setting, or from a textbook.

Developing the new view of preparing a course for Internet delivery

One of the problems with translating face-to-face teaching into alternative modes is that the materials developed for face-to-face teaching actually lack content. These materials are structured, but in the form of a skeleton. There is agreement between the structure that appears in the teachers' handbook and the learners' workbook, but that is all there is: a structure. The structure or skeleton is to be fleshed out by the information that the teacher's notes prompt the teacher to provide to the learner, in class. The learner's notes will be fleshed out by the information provided by the teacher, in class As a result if you take the teacher handbook and the learner workbook you end up with a structural view of the course without content. But at least you have a structure and that is a starting point.

The preferred starting point is with a 'clean sheet' of paper: reversioning or revising existing materials is full of problems. With the clean sheet of paper, the objectives, learning outcomes, competency statements associated with the course can be laid out. If you have a view of what the learner is to achieve, then you should be able to work through the content and develop a structure for the information in the course based on the attributes.

The ability to structure the content based on the outcomes for the learner is one means of creating more sophisticated teaching and learning materials. A further level of analysis on the course material will lead to the possibility of identifying attributes for the information in the course. This could be a schematic diagram of the relationship between elements in the course material. This development of a set of attributes will provide a more meaningful framework for the information (or content) of that attribute and the relationship to the learner's current knowledge. In particular it will open possibilities for the learner to navigate the material. What follows is a listing of the most common attributes of course material. These attributes relate to the content, the means of exposition of the content and the instructional devices that represent the manner of exploring the content. In giving course material an attribute you are verifying that the information has a place in the course. You are also making clear for the learner the relationship between components of the course.

The Internet and instructional design: attributes of the content

It is assumed that course design and outcomes should relate to national training agenda statements and requirements such as NVQs in the UK or similar standards such as the Australian Vocational Training Standards (AVTS), key competencies in language, maths, the sciences and the arts, evolving in countries around the world. If you are planning and preparing an existing course for delivery on the Internet, an underlying assumption is that the instructional design considerations for this course have been undertaken and will be appropriate for the Internet. If this is not the case, you will need to identify the attributes in the course and the appropriate teaching and learning strategies or instructional devices and relate them to the outcomes sought by learners and accrediting agencies. Most learners using the Internet are 'schooled' in the use of course attributes: their schooling was formal. For these people, with a variety of learning styles, to use a textbook involves certain behaviours of access from linear (starting at page one) to eclectic, using the contents page and the index as a means of finding the information they need. It is tempting to use the same paradigm for course material to be delivered on the Internet. This fits neatly with the current vogue to publish on the Internet.

A course has contents and attributes

The course contents have attributes that enable the information in the course to be identified. This identification process can then be matched to the attributes that promote learning in a meaningful manner. One way of identifying the attributes of a course is to deconstruct it into the identifying elements. The terminology will vary in different educational and training settings, but one means of doing this is as follows.

A *course* is made up of *subjects* and/or *modules*. These subjects will have *parts* or *sections*. Within these sections there may be one or several *concepts* that form the basis of the section.

This is one way of deconstructing the content and providing the *elements of information* to form the basis of an Internet version of the content. For example:

> *An element of information*
> An element of information could be as small as a *sentence* or as large as a *section*. It could be a *definition*. In most cases, however, an element of information will be a *paragraph* or *sequence of paragraphs containing a single concept*. There may be *relationships* with other paragraphs that give added meaning.

Identifying these elements and determining the links or relationship with other concepts or activities should provide a dynamic presentation of information to help the learner follow their investigations and learn.

While there are attributes to the course, there are also attributes to delivering a course. This will require consideration of instructional strategies to optimize the use of the technology, which might include modal analysis (see p.21).

Instructional attributes or devices

If the courses you are dealing with already exist, an underlying assumption is that the instructional design considerations for this course have been undertaken. In other words, the needs, expected outcomes, information and tasks for the learner have been identified and appropriate teaching and learning information and activities along with assessment tasks have been developed. This may not directly translate to an Internet delivery. At the same time, if you are developing a new course for delivery via the Internet, you will need to undergo an analysis process about the course and the use of the Internet outlined above.

To present material on the Internet as a learning tool we should be incorporating all those features that optimize computer-based learning and reduce to a minimum those features that have already been identified as hindering learning through the use of computers.

There are probably five styles of presentation. These styles would accommodate the delivery of content taking into account the attributes of the content. These attributes can be classified as:

Theory
    concept to examples
    concrete to abstract
    case studies
Preparation for practice
Simulation and
Problem solving

One of the main features of making Internet-based learning attractive is developing the interaction with the teaching and learning materials.

Strengths

The strengths of computer-based education and training which can be brought to an Internet delivery are:

Educational

➡ ability to work on course at a time convenient to the learner improves motivation;

➡ the 'patience' of the computer when testing and retesting learners for appropriate drill and knowledge;

➡ structured nature of computer-based materials gives learners the view of the content as a professional would view the content;

➡ ability to provide simulations prior to real-world experience provides a learning environment and saves expensive equipment or consumables;

➡ segments of course offered on computer provide variety, may stimulate learners and promote positive attitudes to learning;

➡ courses originating from a central source mean that content versions are minimized, quality is controllable, and reporting, evaluation and record-keeping may be facilitated;

➡ a degree of individualized instruction is possible particularly if the learner is able to navigate the content; and

➡ when properly constructed the computer-based learning is able to provide almost instant feedback.

A further consideration provided by the Internet is the ready availability of links to other sources of information and the ability to send messages. For example, in an engineering course it is possible to point the learner to catalogues or at least e-mail addresses as a source of information for the learner to complete their task.

Weaknesses

Educational

➡ putting material that is not appropriate into computer (electronic page-turning). Possibly this is related to design issues;

➡ interactivity requires both the learner and the notional teacher to actively use the facilities and options provided. Sometimes this does not happen. If there is no interaction there is no communication. But more importantly this is evidence of no commitment to the use of technology.

Technical

➡ limitations such as computer power or screen size or ability of operating system to cope.

Devices

To make the information interactive will require the use one or more of the following devices. These should be used appropriately and in a meaningful relation with the elements of information within the teaching and learning materials. They should be used in a uniform manner in a course or suite of courses. In principle the devices provide a focus for the learner, access to information about available teaching and learning materials and a means of accessing the material in a teaching and learning context that has the potential for accreditation for the learner on completion of the learning tasks.

These devices are:

Statements of objectives, competencies to be achieved and desired outcomes;
Consultations with learners or representatives to determine expected outcomes;
Definitions of terms and concepts;
Sequencing instruction to follow the practice of the expert;

Embedding organizational links in the material to allow or encourage the learner to explore;

Organizers to place the new material with the knowledge and skills already held by the learner;

The placement of questions to encourage learning behaviour and to prompt the learner;

Providing maps (road maps or flow diagrams) of the content, making relationships between concepts apparent or possible courses of action apparent;

Illustrations, graphs and graphics, photographs and audio and video;

Visual signposts, icons, headings, highlighting and pop-ups;

Assessment methods;

Tables;

Simulation and virtual reality;

Practical/workshop/hands on.

Attributes or devices work in the following ways.

Statements of objectives, competencies to be achieved and desired outcomes

Statements of objectives, competencies and outcomes tell course developers of the information required for the learner to achieve the desired outcomes. If these are made known to the learner they provide them with clues about the direction of their enquiry and the information they seek. Making these statements available encourage the learner to consider their current knowledge and skill levels. This encourages the learner and the teaching institute or industrial enterprise to focus on what the learner knows and what they need to know.

Consultation with learners or representatives

This allows the learners to define their learning requirements. In doing so they also start on the learning process. I have included the term representative here because in some cases, at the enterprise level, management and employee representatives may also be stakeholders in the education and training process. In a different case it could be parents, carers or partners who have a legitimate role in the negotiated learning process.

Definitions of terms and concepts

Definitions are discrete information. A definition may be the lowest common denominator as an element of information. In the Internet context of hyperlinks it may also form a point of departure on an exploration on the related teaching and learning materials or an extended search for related information on the Internet.

Sequencing instruction: relationships between elements of knowledge and skills

It is possible to sequence information. The rule to remember is what does the learner need to know before they can come to terms with this new information. How is this knowledge or skill information related to existing knowledge or skills?

Embedding organizers in the text

Organizers are sections of text that tell the learner what they are about to be shown as learning materials. One form of organizer is the advance organizer: this is a summary of the work the learner is about to see. In an Internet delivery this would contain 'hot-spots' to allow interaction and facilitate navigation.

The accepted organizers of a contents page and an index are also available for Internet delivery of teaching and learning material. Again it will be the links created from these that make the Internet material accessible to the learner.

Questions and prompts encouraging learning behaviour

Questions should be set into the text or other means of delivery, that relate directly to the information the learner has just seen and for them to answer at that point. This should serve to embed the new information in the mind of the learner.

Prompts are statements that inform the learner they should recall prior information to use with the new information that is about to be presented to them.

Providing maps (road maps or flow diagrams) of the content, making relationships between concepts apparent

In all courses it should be possible to map the relationship of the concepts in relation to each other. A 'simplified' version of that map may assist a learner with conceptualizing not only the relationship but what they have learned, how it fits in with other concepts and what is still to be learned. A map could be a flow diagram.

As print material, teaching and learning information has a linear sequence, although it is possible to access the information by randomly flicking through the pages of the text. In an Internet version of material it might be advisable to provide a concept map of the information, to tell learners where they are and what information they should access next. This could be in the form of a diagram that alters as major sections of the work are accessed. For example, Figure 4.1 might be the map a learner sees at an early stage of the course.

This would change to the Figure 4.2 (p.56) after the learner has completed the Part One modules. The map would change when the learner reached each identified module or part of the course.

Teaching and learning illustrations, graphs and graphics, photographs and audio and video

On the Internet it is possible for teaching and learning materials to contain these non-text elements. One major consideration will be what problems might be caused to the learner if their machine is not powerful enough or suitably equipped to cope with the demands of a video clip. It is also important that the illustration, video clip (audio-visual element) is linked into the text material and the teaching and learning purpose of the material. While this is a technology problem there are possible solutions such as allowing the learner to download the whole file through their browser. This should enable them to 'run' the file from their hard disc through their browser. The Internet is an

evolving entity and with advances in compression techno
problems of graphics, audio and video will be yesterday's p

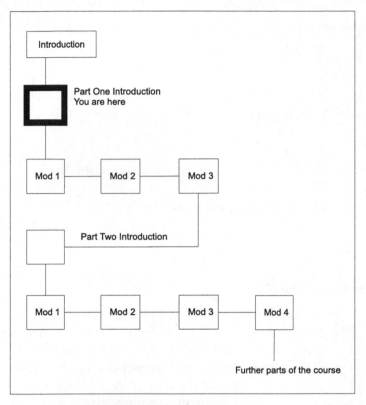

Figure 4.1   Course map 1

Assessment methods

Assessment methods are another device through which learners organize their learning activities. This starts with the learner's concerns about what will be on the test or exam, but is also determined by the need to make submissions during the learning process. So learners may make use of assessment advice as a means of organizing their learning.

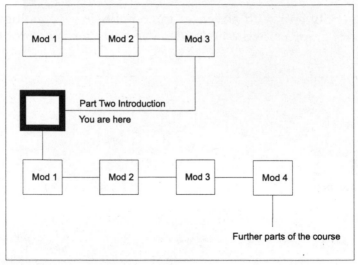

Figure 4.2   Course map 2

Visual sign posts

In many distance education and open learning texts, icons are used to indicate to the learner that information, stills and video are associated with the current material. In these cases the icons refer to material not in the printed text. In an Internet-delivered course some of this information will be available on screen. Clicking on the icon should reveal or *pop-up* the hidden information, visual-audio clip, etc. This hidden material may have other information associated with it.

Headings provide textual clues to the learner. For example these three sets of heading indicate (or should indicate) a level of importance to the information contained under the heading. In most cases a set of headings as set out below will contain the following:

First order or major heading
The key concept or main point(s)

Second order or section headings
Supporting points or illustrative material

Third order or subheadings
Tease out the more subtle points that are the difference
between pretender and expert.

Highlighting of text can assist learners; but it must be consistent if used
as a navigation tool or an indicator of further 'hidden' information.

Tables

These may be used to provide information or as part of a worked
example or an assessment task. In an Internet delivery the use of tables
could be a downloaded task, an interactive task or a developmental
task to be submitted. In the downloaded or developmental task, over
a period of time the learner would construct a table of comparisons to
illustrate their comprehension of variations. In the interactive task a
learner would be dealing in real time with the information in the table.
In this sense the table would be providing a simulation.

Simulation and virtual reality

A simulation is an event where a learner is presented with
information and can input responses or information to achieve an
outcome. For example, there are computer-based learning packages
for training in the use of spreadsheets. When a learner uses one of these
packages and is successful these results need to be recorded. The
outcome should be able to be matched against a 'correct' or 'range of
correct' answers. In more sophisticated forms the simulation may use
animation, audio and video clips. The move into virtual reality is
simulation with a greater degree of reality. The costs of moving into
virtual reality will be related to the complexity of the simulation.

Increasingly it will be possible to use simulation, particularly if
course designers are able to see the educational need. Developers will
need to overcome the desire to develop a virtual reality 'star wars'
bent, and to produce 3D walk-through that will act as vicarious
learning experiences. It is already possible to work in the real world
as a simulation using real data with real outcomes. However, it is safer
in an educational and training environment to be isolated from the
real world for training purposes. At the very least this means that
simulation virtual working does not corrupt the real transactions.

Practical/workshop/hands on

The monitoring of practicals to provide the sanctioning of learning on the Internet is possible. However, when planning the materials and it is apparent that practical activities are required, there will be a need for this requirement to be addressed and a realistic solution to be referred to in the material. This means notifying learners about:

➡ the assessment of these activities;
➡ when and how the assessments are scheduled;
➡ how to arrange to be assessed;
➡ if assessment means attending an assessment centre.

Evaluation tasks

Using the Internet as a teaching and learning tool requires a modification on the approach taken for assessing learner progress in face-to-face teaching. Learners using the Internet may be ready to undertake assessment tasks at different times. This raises the obvious need to have a range of tests available to overcome the possibility of learners comparing tests.

The most appropriate type of evaluation tasks for the Internet involve the use of *check the correct answer/multiple-choice* type activities. These type of test items allow for a large number of variant test items to be developed relating to specific learning outcomes and the ability of these to be placed in a random test generator. It also allows the responses to be corrected automatically and the results 'posted' to the electronic record of the learner held by the institution and to the teacher and the learner for their information.

Where the use of *free text* is required, as in a short answer, a comment or a short essay, these types of responses are best treated as mail messages and directed to the person responsible for evaluating the answers. Currently the development of a thesaurus to cope with free text responses is too time-consuming for a cost-benefit effect over the scanning of the text by the person responsible for assessing the response submitted by the learner.

Reporting

In part this is covered in evaluation tasks above. There are three audiences for *reports* on learner progress. These are the learner, the teacher and the enrolling institution records. If a learner is using Internet delivery, these three audiences will remain. However, the collection of information should be developed so that there are a minimum of extra actions required by the learner, the teacher and the institution to maintain records of the learner's activities, the outcomes and current status. For example, is it possible to forward the results of a learner's submission after it has been assessed, either through a computer-based records management system application or via the assessor to the teacher, the enrolling institution records database and the learner?

Communications

Forms, e-mail, phone, fax and snail mail (see Chapter 5 for more detail on forms) Forms fall into three categories, each designed so that the learner is able to submit information in a manner that is uniform for the purpose. The three generic forms are:

- ➡ enquiry/enrolment;
- ➡ submission of structured test items/multiple-choice/selection, and
- ➡ request/free text/submission.

In the era of electronic forms it is preferable to have one form that evolves, rather than a proliferation of forms that mimic the numerous paper forms required in the past. The fields that you develop for these forms will follow a pattern. All forms will contain fields for names and contact details. However, when a learner enrols, further information fields are added. These will include unique learner identifier, course name, code, teacher involved/contact person/contact position. Note: on enquiry/enrolment forms it is better to have a contact position such as enrolling officer, rather than the name of a particular person because people move more regularly than positions change.

Enquiry/enrolment

Forms for enrolment may have fields for preference of course (if offered) and should include personal detail capture fields for information such as addresses and telephone contacts. It may be an advantage to include fields that allow the capture of information for statistical or reporting purposes to funding bodies such as government departments. This raises other issues of confidentiality.

Submission of structured test items/multiple-choice/selection

Forms for structured test items as well as identification fields will also have fields for questions. These should be able to be generated from an item bank. Questions generated from an item bank require verification of validity. The item bank needs to be large enough to enable random generation of items with variety to cover the course in order that all learners receive a set of questions that contain similar degrees of difficulty while maintaining a variety in challenge to the learner. These forms should also have the capability of being passed through an evaluation application for scoring purposes.

Request/free text/submission

Forms for non-standard requests and free text answers should be able to be submitted to the appropriate teacher through an *e-mail* style facility. In the case of these forms it will be the responsibility of the teacher to respond to the request or assess the free text answers.

The use of *fax* and *phone* contacts and *snail mail* or the *postal service* should not be overlooked as alternative means of communication. Some of these forms of communication may serve the learner's needs better than a dogmatic need to comply with computer-based communication.

Video and audio

This is the most rapidly developing area of the Internet. Consideration will need to given to whether video and audio form part of the course materials. Given the wide range of computer configurations it is difficult to make a prescriptive guide. However, in the immediate future, it may be more appropriate to distribute high-quality video and audio by cassette through the post than have learners using low-speed modem lines. However, the use of emerging desktop video systems (at a cheap price – under $600 AUS) should not be discounted especially as most new computers are being delivered with sound and video cards. These desktop video and audio systems use the technology developed for 'Stump Cam' in cricket, 'Fender Cam' or 'Helmet Cam' in motor racing and yachting. The cameras serve as both face cameras and document cameras.

The current technology has been criticized as it is seen as slow scan screen refresh. However, if the critics could look beyond their 'It is not as good as broadcast' mentality they would see that there are attributes of slow refresh time. For a start, the use of this video can be used in the following settings:

- face-to-face;
- demonstrations;
- explorations.

Face-to-face

The use of desktop video through the Internet could be used for various interview settings. These could be for a job, pre-court hearings with alleged criminals, or between peers in a course, or a course participant seeking information from an expert.

Demonstrations

One criticism of the current video standard is that it blurs movement. In my opinion this is a strength. For example, the blurring of movement in a demonstration allows me to see the path of the hand as it moves through the demonstration.

Explorations

In an interactive setting the blurring motion allows me to sit back and check the thinking of the learner as they work through the problem and vocalize and demonstrate their enquiry process. A less viable alternative solution which still has educational effect is to incorporate captured stills into the information with links in the text of a generic HTML presentation. The advent of an application such as

'HOT JAVA' is an indication of things to come in terms of interaction, simulation and communication.

The wider distribution of servers should mean that this information can be downloaded to a local (campus) server and increase the learners access at minimal connect cost. However, this leaves open the question of selecting appropriate material for delivery using the Internet as a tool. The next section of this chapter examines two scenarios. The first is the conversion of existing materials, the second is the development of new materials.

Selection of appropriate course content

In determining the type of course to be presented and delivered on the Internet there are two possibilities. The first is that the course material already exists, the second is that the course material needs to be developed. In the discussion that follows there are two scenarios based on the existence of the course.

One scenario is that there are existing course materials This means that the analysis of the needs, outcomes and content have been agreed. These assumptions need to be reassessed in relation to delivery of the materials on the Internet. If the course materials and content are appropriate there are still the issues of how best to utilize the attributes of the Internet and to explore other options where it is apparent that the Internet is not suited as a means of delivery.

The second scenario is that the course does exist but the materials are not in a form that is readily transferable to an Internet delivery. Therefore there are no materials. This raises the question of how an Internet delivery might be developed that is beneficial to teachers, learners and the community when developed.

This section examines the following issues:

➡ How do you determine if a course could be suited for development and delivery on the Internet?
➡ Sequencing information: The book as a model;
➡ Characteristics of the Internet for new course delivery;
➡ Sequencing information on the Internet; and
➡ Elements of information.

How do you determine if a course could be suited to development and delivery on the Internet?

In educational and training organizations most of the accredited course material currently available is in print form and skeletal outline. The teachers translate the outline into classroom teaching and learning outcomes. There is an expectation that a teacher working in a classroom will interpret the curriculum documents and present their version of the course with a combination of diagrams, illustrations and photographs, perhaps with a supporting video. How is this transferred to the Internet?

The short answer is that it is possible to transfer everything to the Internet. However, to do so is to fall into the worst trap of electronically delivered material, which is to create course materials that are electronic page-turning with none of the features to encourage learning in a computer environment.

The question you need to ask is: What is the internal logic of the course material that learners need to know? To answer that question you need to consider the following:

➡ How are the outcomes for learners, the objectives, the competencies expected for the learner stated? If these are obvious, you will then have to determine how the content of the course can be given attributes;

➡ You will have to determine attributes for the information;

➡ You will have to determine the links between these elements of information.

At the beginning of this chapter it was stated that a course is made up of subjects and/or modules. These subjects will have parts (sections). Within these sections there may be one or several concepts that form the basis of the section. These can be the means of deconstructing the print version and providing the elements to build the Internet version of the content. To build the Internet version you will need to develop an identifier to cover all the material that can be given a unique identifier to each of the elements. Identifying these attributes enables a more flexible enquiry routine (almost like the routine of using an index in a book) by the learner. This flexible enquiry should support the learner in charge of their learning. One way of comparing existing print materials to materials for the Internet is shown in the following diagram

Sequencing information: The book as a model

If the analogy of a book is used, the following similarities between presenting a course on the Internet and a book arise.

Level One	Title of a course is similar to a textbook title
	List of subjects or modules in a course are similar to the table of contents in a textbook
	Contents in subjects and modules of a course are similar to contents of chapters or sections in a textbook
Level Two	In current course materials it is rare to have an index of contents similar to a textbook
Level Three	There may be references in a course and these are similar to the references in a textbook

Figure 4.3   Structure in print materials

To a large extent the major difference between preparing material for a book and preparing information for the Internet is to be found at Level Two. If you want to prepare information for the Internet as a traditional course, a major consideration will be to determine the finite bits of information and develop the relationship and attributes these bits of information may need to take. The activity that needs to undertaken by a person or team seeking to place learning materials on the Internet is to determine a sequence or links between the information to allow for the learner access to information and to consider alternative pathways to allow for individual learning difference needs or information requirements.

However, if the intention is to provide a source of information and to allow the enquirer or learner to develop their own meaning, then you will need to develop a different set of attributes and a learner-centred means of dealing with the interactions required.

Elements of information (possible attributes)

An element of information could be as small as a sentence or as large as a section. In most cases, however, an element of information will be a paragraph or a sequence of paragraphs containing a single concept. There may be relationships with other paragraphs that give added meaning.

In developing a face-to-face presentation for learners, the intention is to identify these elements and determine the links that should provide a dynamic presentation of information and enable the learner to learn. In order to build the Internet version with a teacher-to-learner orientation, you will need to develop an identifier unique to each of the elements in the material. The attributes will include those of *heading*, or *definition*, or *reading*, or *activity*, or *revision*, among others. Labelling that element of information with an attribute does not mean it is uniquely identified. After all, there may be many elements of information within a course with the attribute *heading*. To further define the element, it will need to have a relationship to other information elements and the attributes of those elements. This is also important for the presentation on screen. If the presentation of the course material is to be dominated by the institution, there are some considerations of labelling the elements to lock the structure. Essentially these are similar to computer-based learning strategies. In this setting the designers of the course will want to label and make links between labels so that the structure of the course follows the understanding of the subject-matter expert.

In this context if you plan to design the presentation you will follow a path as follows.

Page content and links within and between pages

If you are planning a teacher/subject-expert delivery of course materials you will need to identify each specific element of content. There are many ways of doing this. The important point for developers is to maintain the protocol of identification during the planning, development and delivery process.

As an example, it is possible for the course developers to create a set of identifiers for information in a course, or activities in a course, and provide information about the links so that a programmer is able to prepare a course and the links between these elements in a course. This will mean the development of a set of codes so that the crosslinks between the pages of information are documented. The reason for this documentation may seem trivial when you first develop the information. The documentation will become very important if there is ever a subsequent need to revise the course.

For example:

➡ a code 'S' for learner/general information; or
➡ 'T' exclusively for teacher information;
➡ a code for the course, eg, 'UBP' for the subject Urban Planning;
➡ a code for the module, eg, 'STAN' for the module Statistical Analysis;
➡ a unique code for the element of information. This might be a logical reference to the location of the material in the original information.

As a result you arrive at a code for a specific piece of information such as:

UBPSTAN004, where 004 is the location of the information.

For another piece of information it might be identified as:

UBPKNT004, in this instance much of the identifier seems the same except for the code change KNT. This indicates that the information comes from the KNT module of the course.

This type of identifying and cross-referencing is fine if the product is to be a computer-based education and training package and for the programmer developing the package. But what about the learner? Do they want to know that they need to address UBPSTAN004 in order to get information from the STAN part of the course?

In an enquiry-driven version of a course on the Internet the learner is looking for materials that they can utilize to build their skills for their immediate need. For these people the navigational devices need to be menus and perhaps icons and hot spots in text to allow them to work their way through the material. This working may seem haphazard to a teacher if it does not follow the learning path the teacher expected. Given the 'model' of the Internet as source of information, with the learners making of that information what they will, the haphazard, eclectic activities of learners are only able to be evaluated against a consideration of: Did the learner achieve what they set out to do? This may or may not be for formal recognition. For these people recognition of current skills, consideration of former and formal learning and access to courses to develop a skill set are important only to the extent that they improve their skills, increase the possibility of employment options, gain recognition for qualifications or satisfy a whim.

Considerations about course materials

Most courses consist of practical and theoretical components. Even the most academic courses require the learner to submit a practical submission, such as an essay, to indicate a grasp of the content and to demonstrate their capabilities in arguing/handling the content of the subject. If you are considering developing a version of the course for delivery through the Internet, you will need to determine how you will handle these aspects of the course.

There is a mistaken belief that the handling of theoretical material seems less of a problem. There seems to be a general opinion that course developers for an Internet delivery will initially want to consider how they will handle the practical aspects of the course. If I follow the line of argument that dealing with practical activities are an issue in the delivery of course material on the Internet, the following considerations may arise.

Practicals

Where a course has a practical component, you will need to decide what actions the learner needs to take to demonstrate that the learner is competent. In the first instance, consideration should be given to including information of the objectives and expected out-comes and assessment scheme of any practical work as a guide within the theoretical component. This could also include information for the learner to seek advance standing either through a recognition of their current abilities or through a recognition of equivalent studies.

You will need to ask the question

You will need to consider whether the learners need to attend a weekend session or after-hours session to demonstrate their practical abilities.

You may consider that other options are equally valid and open as an assessment to enable a learner to demonstrate their competencies. Some of these may seem radical but they may form an option that is both valid and economical for the learner and the teacher.

For example:

➡ Is it possible to present a simulation scenario to encourage the learner to practise prior to, or as remediation after, a practical?
➡ Is it possible for the learner to bring examples of their work from the workplace?
➡ Is it possible for the learner's workplace supervisor to provide a statement about the ability of the learner?

These are directly related to the practical components of a course and may fit in with other aspects of course delivery being promoted by the educational and training institution, such as:

➡ granting of advanced standing;
➡ recognition of prior learning;
➡ accelerated progression.

The important consideration, at the design stage of any delivery, but in this case an Internet delivery, is how to devise activities within the Internet delivery to sanction the practical components of a course.

An example: How would you get learners working through the Internet to demonstrate they could carry out mouth-to-mouth resuscitation?

(a) They write out a checklist;

(b) They demonstrate in front of an adult;

(c) They demonstrate in front a supervisor;

(d) They demonstrate in front of a person with first-aid qualifications.

But:

(e) What happens if the learner already has a first-aid certificate?

Or:

(f) What happens if you examine other areas of the course or the expressed interest of the learner and find out that they need to do bandages, the lifting of casualties or the suppression of bleeding?

If the requirement of the learner is general first aid then none of (a), (b) or (c) serve a purpose. The option (d) could overcome the immediate verification problem but what of the other learner needs?

The part of the scenario at (e) seems to be straightforward. Give them recognition for prior learning. However, before that can happen there will need to be actions to determine that the prior qualifications reflect current practices and standards, that the learner is a competent practitioner, not just a holder of a certificate: in other words, that they are up to date.

The opportunity offered by scenario (f) includes requiring the learner to complete a first-aid course that satisfies all the requirements and to recognize this as equivalent to at least the practical part of the course or learner's need and accelerate the progression of the learner.

It is also important that considerations about the learner to demonstrate practical skills are related to the underlying concepts or theory. In an Internet delivery of a course there will need to be consideration about the form of theory presentation. There is the paradigm of classroom or didactic presentation represented by teachers and gatekeepers of knowledge. There is also the more eclectic, enquiry-based consideration of learners as active negotiators in developing access to the learning and information they require.

Considerations for the theoretical components of the course

In the classroom, using a white board and felt pen or only using overheads (chalk and talk) is not the most stimulating means of conveying theory. The use of the Internet requires that a selection process takes place.

Some of the questions you will need to ask about presenting the theory component of a course or a theory-based course are:

→ What in this material is most appropriate for presentation and delivery to learners by the Internet – ie a computer?
→ What in the content will promote interaction with the content?
→ What in the content requires learner input, such as selection from multiple-choice possibilities?
→ Most of the course material currently available is in print form, perhaps with a supporting video. How is this transferred to the Internet?

If you assume that the Internet is an open-learning space and you are using the Internet as a delivery tool then the following questions should be answered by you as a developer. As stated earlier, a needs analysis should have provided you with answers to questions such as:

→ Who might be searching for your information?
→ How do you sanction any learning or 'claim' to learning?

Then there are considerations of the learner

If a learner is going to access teaching and learning materials through a computer, certain considerations at the planning stage might assist the learner. One of the first considerations is the use of a *help* facility. This is discussed in Chapter 6. I can only write the obvious here: I consider a help facility that offers no help to be no help.

Then there are the possibilities of supporting the accelerated progression of the learner. This aspect of the use of the Internet needs to be explored. With course material available on the Internet, a learner might be able to take at least two actions to improve their standing within the course. The first is to request and after the submission of documents achieve recognition for prior learning, or work-related learning that links to the course. One feature that recognition systems are keen to promote is that prior learning or experience will be taken into account to break the traditional time-serving structure of educa-tion and training. However, as a generalization, the overlay of docu-mentation to 'prove' prior learning or experience and a grant of recognition seems to be more than attending the course or subject. Yet through an appropriate Internet interface much of this documentation could be easily managed.

A second possibility is that the learner could elect for a pre-test. This pre-test would cover aspects of the course. On submitting the results and after analysis the learner would be forwarded a report about their study needs in relation to the course. This might serve as a means of accelerating some learners through the course. The use of such tests might also include the use of simulations, where the simulation gives a wider perspective on the learner's capability.

A further aid to the learner would be to provide them (and you) with an audit trail of what the learner accessed prior to taking the test to determine if the learner failed because of bad access skills on their part, bad design on your part or what the learner needs to do as remediation.

Another consideration for the learner is access time costs. If the learner is working with a local server, time costs are minimal but important. If the learner is working from a remote site, consideration should be given to the ability to download the material. This will means considerations of security of the materials and of the learner's interaction back to the site.

Course delivery on the Internet

The Internet is promoted as a superhighway of information. In reality it is a conduit for people seeking information and/or course materials. The Internet is not neutral as a conduit in that the perform-ance available to the person using the Internet is a product of the design of the course material, the computer power supporting that material and the computer power of the learner's own computer.

The facility of the Internet is also dependent on the type of browser and enquiry structures available to the learner. Your course design for presentation on the Internet might not be very user friendly if the user is accessing the course on a slow modem, with a different browser and from the opposite side of the country or hemisphere.

There is also an issue of confidence for both the promoters of a course, the institutions offering course materials and the learners seeking access. Each of these will be questioning the credibility of a course delivered by the Internet. In any new venture or means of course delivery there will be doubts about the material and the means of delivery. The question all developers ask is: 'Will it work?' This is an understandable question of confidence.

In the short term, developers of courses for delivery via the Internet will have to face the question of confidence not only of the process but of the outcomes in any course development and delivery setting. When it comes to the use of the Internet as a delivery tool there are different perspectives. The current mythology of the Internet is that it is an open-access computer-based enquiry and messaging system. This is interpreted by the public as open access to information. But what if the learner wants accreditation? How will learners respond if there are asked to provide evidence about their current skills to satisfy competency standards? How will learners react if this information is to be recorded?

There are two assumptions you can make. The first is that learners accessing your site and information may not require recognition or accreditation. They came, they saw and they went away contented. This may have implications for how you see your intellectual property rights. The second is that the learner will seek some form of acknowledgement for accessing your material. At this point, records, results and course-fee considerations come to the fore. You need to consider these aspects sooner rather than later, not least because you need to think about security arrangements for learners submitting responses to course requirements and personal information including addresses, credit card numbers and phone numbers.

Confidence

Assuming that there is an audience for your information and the mechanisms for sanctioning the learning outcomes, if learners use the course materials on the Internet, it is still possible that questions will be raised about the use of the Internet as a teaching and learning space. This is a question of confidence in the use of the Internet as a delivery tool. This is usually raised by those with a conservative approach to education. It is also a question of confidence that can be raised about any non-face-to-face delivery method.

Ask yourself the following about a learner using a face-to-face delivered course:

➡ Did the learners pass the test?
➡ Did the learner pass the questions set in the test?
➡ Did all the questions cover all aspects of the content?

Now are you prepared to say that the learner is knowledgeable? In reality the question is about the testing procedure not the method of delivery or the learner's ability.

Further confidence test: The learner failed the knowledge test that the learner filled in on an electronic form on a computer in their workplace. However, the learner completed the practical tasks competently. Are you prepared to say that the learner is not competent?

I recognize that these cases seem to be comparing chalk and cheese, but the problem is a real one. The problem is one of perceptions about learners learning and the sanctioning of that learning when it is undertaken in other than conventional settings. I suspect that for many in the educational and training community, learning to use the Internet is another alternative beyond the barely or grudgingly accepted means of course delivery by correspondence.

Conclusion

As there is very little experience of delivering courses via the Internet, one option is to look at similar experiences in delivering courses. The logical choice is that of course delivery by computer. One expectation is that the same strengths and weakness that apply to computer-based learning will apply to most aspects of teaching and learning on the Internet.

The strengths of computer-based education and training that might be brought to an Internet delivery include, among others:

➡ the ability to work on course at a time convenient to the learner either online or by downloading a course or

          components to be worked on in real-time stand alone run
          time;

➡ the structured nature of computer-based materials
    providing the learner with a professional view of the
    content;

➡ provides simulations prior to real world experience;

➡ possible individualized instruction;

➡ Internet learning is capable of providing almost instant
    feedback.

These strengths are further enhanced when the Internet has a ready availability of links to other sources of information and the ability to send messages.

There are weaknesses, which include:

➡ putting inappropriate material on the Internet;

➡ both the learner and the notional teacher need to actively
    use the facilities and options provided. Sometimes this
    does not happen. If there is no interaction there is no
    communication. If there is no communication it is difficult
    to verify that learning is taking place.

These are not the only considerations. Currently, computer-based tools are available that allow the direct conversion of word-processed files to pages on the Internet. But more than just a simple conversion of format is needed to make text material suitable for educational and training use on the Internet. What is required is a process of analysis to make sure that the materials that go on the Internet are quality teaching and learning materials, that will engage the learner in meaningful teaching and learning activities. This means developing a more sophisticated structure to the materials.

Structuring the content on the basis of intended learning outcomes or objectives is one means of creating more sophisticated teaching and learning materials. A further level of analysis on the course material will lead to the possibility of identifying attributes for the information in the course. It is the development of a set of attributes that will provide a more meaningful framework for the information (or content) of that attribute. These attributes, or the relationship between attributes, will indicate ways of presenting the content and the instructional devices that represent the manner of exploring the content.

These along with the requirement of the learner, are indicators of how material could be presented to satisfy course presentation and the enquiry of an individual learner.

For general considerations of course development see Forsyth *et al.* (1995) *Planning a Course, Preparing a Course, Delivering a Course* and *Evaluating a Course* (Kogan Page, London). These are four interrelated books that consider the issues at each stage of course development and delivery. The books address the issues on analysis and materials production that you will need to consider for any means of course delivery including the use of the Internet.

chapter **5**   **Forms**

Summary

In a world where paper administartion proliferates, the computer offers the option of limiting the need to fill in forms. Unfortunately, many computer applications seem to generate forms. If you are considering using the Internet as a means of delivery of a course and the resultant need to maintain records, then an accretion of fields in a form may be a better strategy than developing a form for each purpose.

In any educational and training setting there is a need for records to be kept and this leads to the need for forms. In this discussion of forms I refer to electronically generated forms that are of use to the learner, the teacher and the educational and training institution. It is not the intention of this chapter to be prescriptive about form design. Form design should relate to the actual need to collect information about learners, their use of the information or applications you provide for them and any unique characteristics of data capture and transmission you need about the course or materials.

Much time and effort can be spent in developing forms. Sometimes these forms do not perform the expected task or capture the needed information. Frequently there is unneeded duplication of data capture. This can be frustrating for the learner, the teacher and the person managing the data collected by the forms.

In this chapter I propose that as a generalization in any use of the Internet to deliver educational and training courses there need only be three generic areas. These areas will cope with:

➤ enquiry/enrolment from potential and enrolling learners;
➤ structured tests/multiple-choice and selection-type responses in an assessment setting; and
➤ request/free text/submission-type of responses from learners.

This chapter examines the three basic areas of a form I have proposed and argues that in fact these might be one form with elaborations or extensions to the field on the form.

Why have only three areas in a form?

First, I do not mean three areas or even three forms are all that will be required. In reality the number of forms, or the fields in a form, that you will need will be dictated by the course materials you are developing and the types of interaction or information you require from the learner. For example, if the course is theory oriented, then it may be inappropriate to have short answer areas in forms because your requirement is for a more considered submission form for the learner. In this case the course may only have two basic areas in the form: the area generated by the enquiry and subsequent enrolment and an area in the form to accept the submission of the learner's free text queries and responses to the assessment tasks of the course.

Common features of all forms

When dealing with course material delivered on the Internet, the three generic areas in the form outlined above should have as a minimum the following information displayed in all subsequent generations of any form. As you will see from the examples, there are subtle differences, but as a general rule the form should have common fields for name, address and contact details.

Please note that the form structure here, is or should be, within the standard Internet screen with the navigational devices at the top and the options at the bottom of the screen. The leading setting for an enquiry form might be as in Figure 5.1.

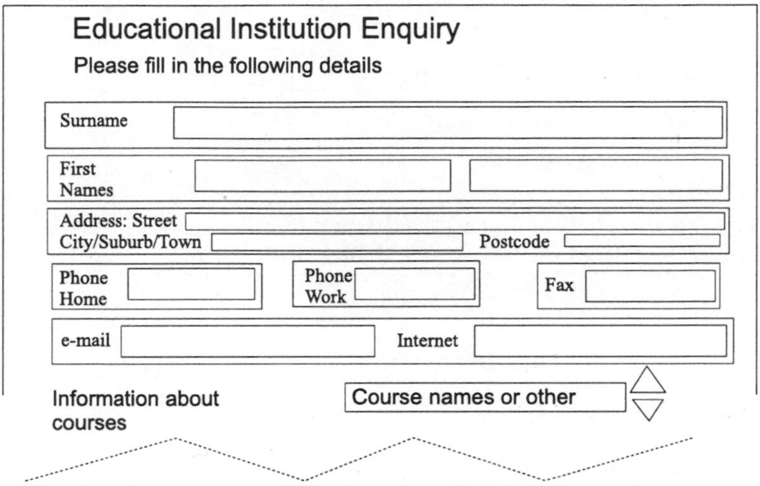

Figure 5.1   An enquiry form

The information collected in this leader is valuable. The submission of this information should generate a unique record identifier and this becomes part of the response. This would form the basis of any further communication with the person making the enquiry. At this level you are in effect developing a closed-user group between that person and the institution.The response should reflect this to the enquirer and there will be changes to the leader to indicate this response.

This reaction generates a second part of the form involving collecting the request, shown in Figure 5.2. Here you will see that a reference number has been added. This should be unique and expands some other fields in the form to collect funds.

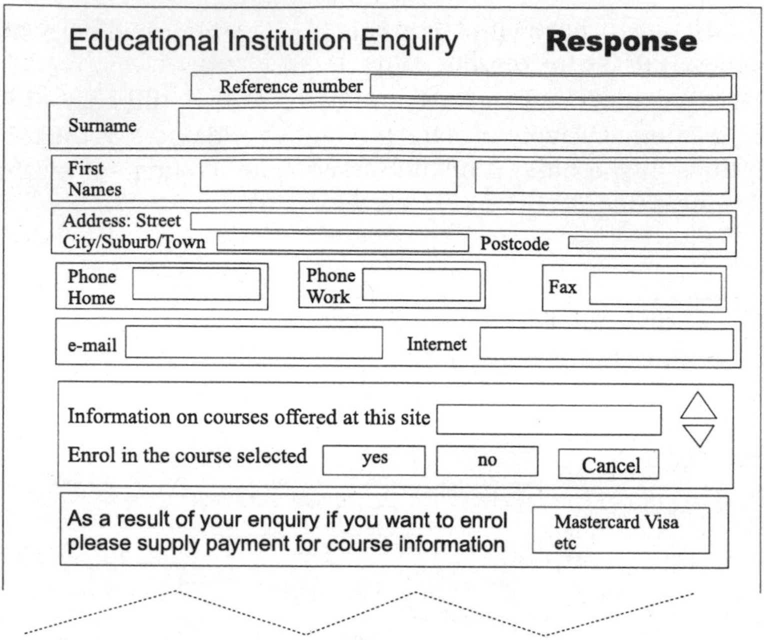

Figure 5.2   A field to allow the collection of funds
is added

The commitment to enrol generates a further field in the leader section. This is to allow you to collect funds. Here I have used the Master-card/Visa example. In the near future these could well be smart cards with credit points issued by education authorities. Whatever type of fee collection your organization is involved with, you will need to make sure that the proper links are in place with the credit-granting institution, bank or credit-card agency The Internet is not a secure transaction environment. There are people who trawl the Internet seeking personal information for their financial benefit. You need to consider the security of your enrolment and submission from student's procedures and protocols.

If the enquirer enrols and becomes a learner they should be assigned a contact person or teacher. This should appear in all subsequent Internet dealings by the learner and the teacher. This should become part of the leader of either an enquiry or assessment task form. Note that the original information submitted with the original enquiry has been carried through. An example of this accretion of recognized information to the form is illustrated in Figure 5.3, where the course name, number and learner identification are added.

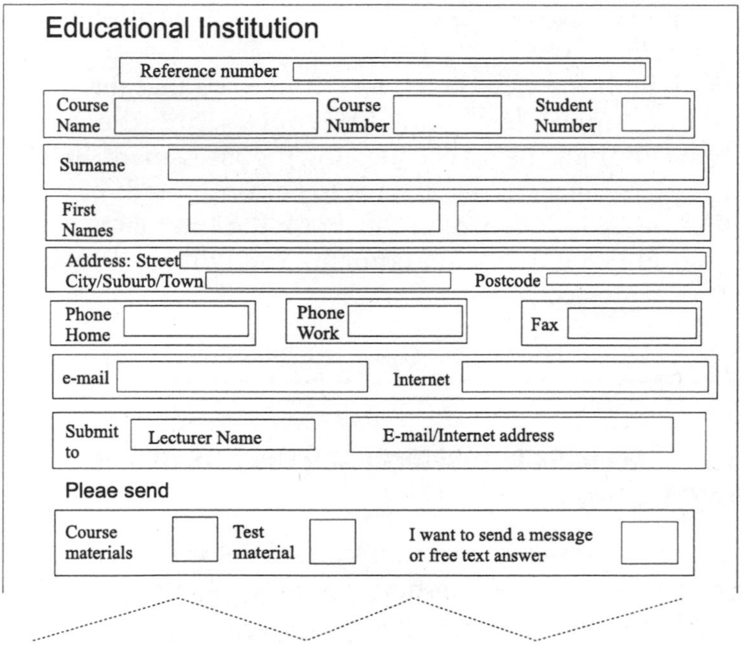

Figure 5.3   Learner's enrolment validated

Having made the request for either course materials, test materials or to send a message or submit a free text answer to a question, the two other types of form are generated. These will be the short answer and/or free text forms.

Three Notes

➡ The request for course materials is handled as part of a proforma set of dialogue boxes that will be based on the material in the course and it is difficult to demonstrate a generic structure here. One possibility is that the course workbook associated with the computer-based material may be able to be printed out for the learner at this point.

➡ As with the case of delivery it may be that for some assessment tasks the Internet is not the most appropriate means of collecting the assessment. In this case other options will have to be considered.

➡ As stated elsewhere in this book the Internet is not a secure computer environment. You will need to take this into account.

The short answer test form and the free text or request option

It is expected that if the course you are delivering via the Internet is suited for short answer question type assessment tasks, the following should be considered as a minimum:

(1) an item bank of test questions validated and with a significant number of items per test topic to enable the random generation of multiple-choice and click-on-the-box questions;

(2) an application to generate valid tests covering the course content and expected outcomes;

(3) a repository for submitted responses, preferably with an answer-checking application; and

(4) a means of reporting the outcome to the learner, the teacher and to any central learner records.

How you might set out the special fields in each form will depend on the type of information to be collected. However, the header of the form will be modified only minimally to account for the function. All the information in most of the fields will be as collected or generated by the first enquiry and enrolment.

Educational Institution Assessment		Assessment Task Number	

Reference number

Course Name		Course Number		Student Number	

Surname

First Names

Address: Street
City/Suburb/Town　　　　　　　　　　　Postcode

Phone Home		Phone Work		Fax	

e-mail　　　　　　　　Internet

Submit to	Lecturer Name	E-mail/internet address

In this area is generated a multiple-choice/click on the correct response type assessment task generated from an item bank

Figure 5.4   The form as a cover sheet for submitting an assignment

Forms for submitting free text assessment task and requests

The short answer free text test or request

This type of communication has the potential to increase a teachers workload. In many educational and training settings the length of response to a question requiring a free text response need not be too long In some cases three paragraphs might be enough.

In these cases where the free text response is short, an e-mail type response should be satisfactory. However, in the interest of security it may be better to use a form that incorporates data about the learner, see Figure 5.5 below. As such the following is but one example and follows on from the format already established with other forms used between the course provider or teacher communicating with the learner. This has the advantage of being familiar to the learner.

Educational Institution   Free Text Assessment Task Number [   ]

Reference number [   ]

| Course Name [   ] | Course Number [   ] | Student Number [   ] |

Surname [   ]

First Names [   ]   [   ]

Address: Street [   ]
City/Suburb/Town [   ]   Postcode [   ]

| Phone Home [   ] | Phone Work [   ] | Fax [   ] |

e-mail [   ]   Internet [   ]

| Submit to | Lecturer Name | E-mail/Internet address |

In this area is generated a question from an item bank. The learner is expected to draft a free text response and this is submitted via e-mail or the Internet to the teacher for their assessment

Figure 5.5   Free text field in the form

A final word on forms

In this chapter I have said that there really only needs to be one form. I have also said that these forms will evolve over time. The main point of any form you develop when using an electronic means such as the Internet is to minimize the need to duplicate data entry.

Note

In the real world it is relatively easy to incorporate the college, school, university logo/coat of arms. On the Internet these graphical devices can take a lot of time to download and appear on the learner's screen. This can be a source of frustration. Remember the prime use of the forms is for the learner to communicate accurate information to the institution and have accurate information returned.

Conclusion

Electronically generated forms must be of use to the learner, the teacher and the educational and training institution.

Forms play an important role: after all, learners have to be enrolled and information about the learner has to be collected. Form design should relate to the actual need to collect information about learners, their use of the information or applications you provide for them and any unique characteristics of data capture and transmission you need about the course or materials. The good point about many electronic forms is that once you have collected information on the learner and supplied information to them, there is no longer a need to fill out forms.

Any electronic form you develop will need to satisfy the needs of the administration of your institution. The development of a generic form will need to cope with:

➡ enquiry/enrolment from potential and enrolling learners;
➡ structured tests/multiple-choice and selection type responses in an assessment setting; and
➡ request/free text/submission type of responses from learners.

Information provided at the point of enquiry should be stored and carried forward if the learner enrols and as they work on the course materials. The real action of electronic interaction and working with information either online or down loaded from the Internet can take place with a minimum of electronic administrivia.

chapter 6   Specific Considerations

Summary

Teaching and learning materials on the Internet consist of bits of data that become information when the learner has access to and uses the data appropriately in a teaching and learning environment to develop new knowledge, skills and attitudes.

For this to work, the same rigour that is applied to other forms of delivery must be applied to the development of materials for delivery on the Internet.

The structural development of material currently on the Internet seems to be based on text files and occasionally on the use of a database. In the main, these are translations of computer files on to Internet 'pages' using a version of a text markup language such as Hypertext Markup Language (HTML). In many cases the information has had little more than a few identifiers marked or highlighted on keywords. This highlighting is translated by the text markup language as a link. These links allow the user to jump forward (or back) in what is a text file to the linked information. However, in most cases the same information can be accessed or scrolled through the text file using the down arrow or page down or holding the mouse button down on the vertical movement scroll on the right-hand side of the computer screen.

Other applications, tools and devices are being developed for use on the Internet. The best place to find these tools for the development of course materials is on the Internet. The evolution of these tools such as JAVA, then HOT JAVA or even the browsers such as Mosaic, Netscape or Microsoft Internet Explorer, are only part of the evolution of the Internet. With the use of these tools, some interesting Internet sites are developing. However, the developers of these interesting sites must remember that it is the power of the enquirer's computer that makes the site accessible. If the learner does not have a computer, or access to a computer, to run the material offered by the Internet site, they do not have access to the site.

In this treatment of making information available to learners, the ability of the learner to generate an enquiry is limited to the links engineered into a file-linking process by the course developer. This type of course development for use in a computer environment leads to second guessing the possible requests from the learner. Another means of organizing information for presentation on the Internet is the use of a database structure. The attraction of using a database as the foundation for the presentation of course material on the Internet is that data is placed in cells within the database and the learner is then able to gain access to the data through the use of their search-and-enquiry routines. If you want to follow this type of course delivery on the Internet, you need to consider the use of assigning attributes to the elements of information in the course.

What follows is some information about establishing your site, some features of organization and some security issues. Any course delivered on the Internet, whether a translation of an existing course or the development of a new one, must have the same academic rigour and the same integrity as any other delivery version of the course content.

In this chapter the following issues are raised:

> ➡ *Establishing your site*
> How will you determine your structure and access and organize the material for presentation?

➡ *Aspects of help*
➡ *Security*

At the time of development you will need to consider how your computer system will handle learner interaction and the structural and strategy devices for use in teaching and learning materials.

However, in raising them I am only able to offer a generic set of solutions because the solutions should be dictated by content and the learner's access to the content and the ability of the technology (or your technology support people) to facilitate the delivery of content.

Establishing your site

There are many in the Internet community who would say go ahead and do it. The information is available on the Internet and books. Many people have a home page on the Internet. But that is their home page. If you are seeking to establish a home page within an institutional setting, the offering of course material on the Internet has far greater ramifications for the institution, the learners and staff. I have left this consideration to now because I wanted to open up the range of issues before you rush into creating your home page. You need to consider the educational and training rationale for developing materials for Internet delivery on the basis of the educational and training need, not the use of the technology. But by now you are probably at the point of developing your Internet materials and there are some general considerations you need to take into account. You probably have a site on the Internet with a disclaimer that it is a site under construction. Develop and refine your site before going public. This can be done using local area network or even files on the hard disk and the floppy disk drives.

How will you determine your structure and access?

This will depend on the course content and how you choose to make it accessible. To be more helpful, I will outline what I consider to be a suitable structure for delivering material on the Internet and capable of modification according to your educational and training needs, or requests from learners.

In presenting this generic model I assume there is the need to satisfy a demand for a course by delivering part or all of the course material on the Internet. I assume the Internet is a delivery tool available for the instructional need and satisfies access requirements of the learners. I also assume you have been through some of the administration requirements to present the material on the Internet.

Assuming people (possible learners) have an Internet access, there are three possible reasons for them to access your material:

➡ there will the curious browsers;
➡ there will be the browsers who might want to commit to a course; and
➡ there will be those who are already committed.

People will come across your home page either by accident or by enquiry and there are two possible things they may want to do when they reach the home page – or, more correctly, when they have enquired about courses available from your home page.

The first is they will move on in their browse of the Internet. The second is they will want further information or to enrol. The following figures outline some of the features that your home page and associated pages will need to handle.

Figure 6.1 shows two types of people accessing information on the Internet: the active learner looking for a course and the person browsing through home pages on the Internet. The person browsing the Internet should be able to gain information about the course (or courses) being offered at your site and an outline of contents. If they are interested in exploring further, it is probably best for them to send an enquiry or enrol. If they wish to do neither, there should be the navigational devices at all points for them to return to their browsing of the Internet. However, if the person browsing seeks to enrol, they become similar to an active learner.

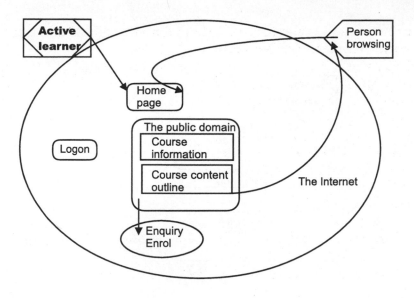

Figure 6.1   A schematic of people accessing the
course

Active learners are looking for a course. They will want to enrol and
they should be able to do so. This will require the generation of forms
that collect data on the learner and a means of paying for the course
if that is required. This is covered in Chapter 5 on Forms. Once this
active learner is enrolled, there is the need to expedite their access to
your site on all subsequent visits. There is nothing more frustrating
for a learner in a computer environment than to have to work through
pages of information they already understand. In order to facilitate
the learner it should be possible for the computing people to establish
an audit trail of the learner as they access the information and this
could be linked to a log-on process to take the learner to the point
where they were last working on the teaching and learning materials.
This is one option. Another option would be to review the structure
of the information. For the active learner the process could be represented as follows. Other people may still browse. This surface level
information is available to all and while this information may be
available to all, you should be careful to protect any commercially
valuable information at this surface level.

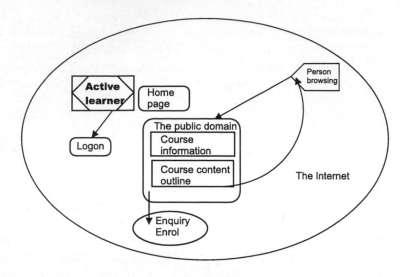

Figure 6.2   The active learner logs on

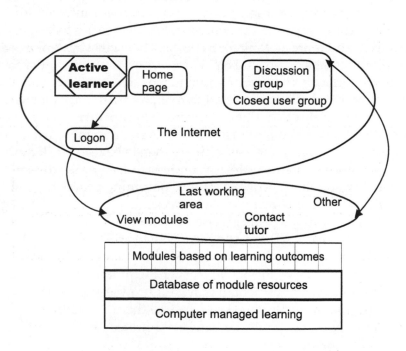

Figure 6.3   Access possibilities for the active learner

When the active learner logs on for the first time it is logical that they be shown a structure similar to the course content available in the public domain. However, as they move through the course and develop their expertise learners may want to control their access to the information as well as take up where they left off.

As soon as the learners are active, their view of the information changes, as shown in Figure 6.3. At this point the active learner is able to access information, resume where they left off, contact their tutor or check on the latest discussion (if any) in the closed-user group associated with the course. I have represented the modules of the course, the database and computer-managed learning, as outside the Internet. This is consistent with the learner downloading the information they need to complete the module or course. However, the modules are based on learning outcomes, statements of competencies to be gained or objectives. In developing an Internet-delivered course these will be the informing elements about how the course information is to be made available or linked to the needs of a learner. An Internet delivered course should be built not on the basis of a face-to-face course but the way a learner may want to access information. This will be learning outcomes, statements of competencies to be gained or objectives and indicate to the learner how they can satisfy the criteria to pass the course.

The underlying structure of sequencing and determining attributes is reflected in the structure of the course materials' presentation.

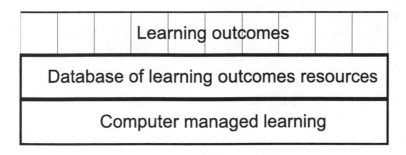

Figure 6.4   The underlying structure

In Figure 6.4 there are ten modules. This is an illustration only: in some courses there may be more, in others less. These modules are supported by a set of resources. It may well happen that some of the module resources are common across more than one module. So it is important to identify this information so that it appears in the database only once, but is appropriately cross-referenced as an element in the database. This element has an attribute that might be used elsewhere.

One of the main benefits of this is that should an element of information change, it only needs to be changed as a data element. This change will be reflected and consistent when a learner works with the module or modules containing that information element.

If a snapshot through this level of course material could be taken, it would have the following:

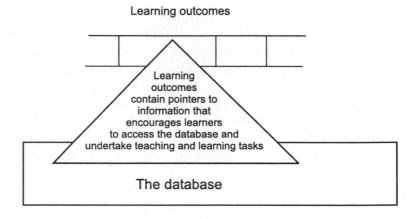

Figure 6.5   The relationship between the learning outcomes and the database

The database has a relationship with the learning outcomes and needs to be kept up to date. However, there is a further matter for maintaining the course material and that is the assessment tasks.

In the model that has been developed in this chapter and set out in Figure 6.3, there is a computer managed learning component.

Figure 6.6 indicates that the database for the course must be related to the information that the learners are accessing. However, there are further possibilities that are not so apparent. For example, it may be that the learner makes a query relating to a learning outcome (read database) and this triggers off a randomly generated question and answer session related to the learner's query. It could be that the result of such an exchange between the learner and the database generates a result that the learner qualifies for course credits because of their prior learning or experience. After all, the power of using computing is in generating learning options. The real problem is that people have to think up inventive ways of making the computer work while maintaining an educational and training outcome.

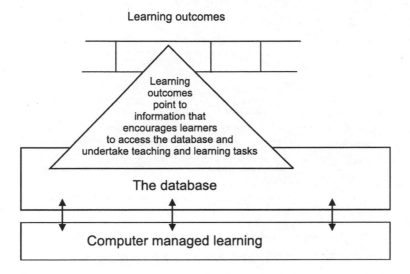

Figure 6.6   Computer managed learning

As Figure 6.7 (p.96) suggests, it should be easy for a learner's responses to be stored outside the Internet. This gives an added protection to these records of the learner's achievement.

The HELP function

There is another aspect of the delivery that you should consider: the help function. This is the most difficult function to organize because if it is offered at one level of the material, it should be offered at all levels.

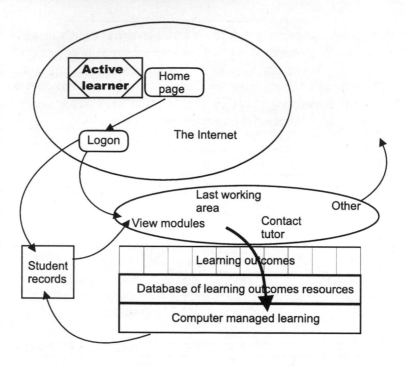

Figure 6.7   Maintaining the learner's records

There is nothing so frustrating as a help function that offers no help. The problem is trying to determine where learners might need help. This second guessing can be minimalized if there is a chance to observe potential users interact with the information. I say users because computer 'experts' may have knowledge that users do not and the expert may find some lack of clarity is easy to overcome by hacking away at the information. In the computing world the term for help functions is context related. In this Internet setting of course delivery the context of help-related information takes three forms:

➡ navigation;
➡ information; and
➡ task completion.

Diagramaticaly the HELP function would look as follows:

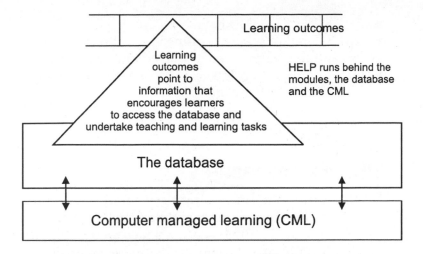

Figure 6.8   The HELP function running behind the teaching and learning materials

Alongside the three factors of navigation, information and task completion there should be a HELP that is a direct link to the tutor. There is one problem with this link which is while the tutor should be able to help with questions about the information and on the assessment tasks, in the short term many tutors will be coming to grips with operating the Internet-delivered course themselves. This inexperience of the tutors will be minimalized if a proper staff development programme is carried out alongside the development of the Internet course.

Aspects of HELP: Navigation

For new learners using the Internet and your course materials it is possible they will have problems in navigation. The problems of navigation on the Internet are probably beyond your course. However, within your course there should be a consistency of using navigational devices. This should be apparent from your home page and in the information and task pages of the course. At least five navigational devices might be needed:

➡ back to home page;

➡ back to the page they have come from;
➡ back to previous predetermined logical page;
➡ forward to the next predetermined logical page; and
➡ forward to the page linked to highlighted text on this page and back from that page.

Therefore, HELP on these navigational tools would be appropriate.

HELP: Course information

HELP on course information presents a problem. If the learner has not understood the information on the screen and clicks on HELP, then in a context-related HELP situation what can the computer do? The computer is only able to supply the information it has been programmed to access. The course-material designer may try and second guess the queries about the information, but the computer is only as good as the programmer. However, over time a computer can store the types of queries for information and this may make the HELP information smarter. But initially you may have to build into the Internet course the fall back position used in face-to-face teaching. That is to have an alternative source stating the same information in a different manner. Or there is the possibility of referring the learner to other sources: learner workbooks or other text sources such as library books. While the Internet allows such expansion of information sources, these sources usually have to be considered at the time of developing the course materials.

HELP: Access to the course teacher/tutor through an e-mail style option

Assessment task completion advice

While there may be a difficulty in second guessing the type of HELP a learner might need when they are working through information it is easier to predict what type of HELP a learner might need when completing an assessment task. Depending on how your course materials are organized, the HELP questions will range from deadlines for submission, possibly claims of hardship (illness, etc), to content-specific queries.

Discussion of features of organizing material for presentation

Home page and screen design

I have left discussion of the home page to this point because the home page generates problems of its own. These are minimalized if your front-end analysis of the course has been thorough.

A home page on the Internet must be all things to all people. Your home page is important in creating a first impression. However, first impressions are like covers on a book and the reader's perception of the content. In other words, an impressive home page requires impressive presentation of contents. It follows that unless these contents meet with the learner's needs and maintain the presentation standards set by the home page, then the perception of those visiting the contents of an impressive and inviting home page may not be as positive about the unassuming pages of content behind the impressive façade.

Screen design

The delivery of course material via the Internet will have many of the attributes of delivering a course in a computer-based learning setting. As such, most of the considerations in relation to screen design will apply to material developed for delivery through the Internet:

- ➡ font size: 12 point minimum;
- ➡ line length: approximately 45 to 55 characters;
- ➡ number of lines: determined by the text, graphics and the content and the need for interaction;
- ➡ background: contrast ratio between background and text;
- ➡ highlights in text: contrast ratio between standard text and highlighted text: colour contrast relating to grey scale;
- ➡ graphics/illustrations: include only when needed and referred to;
- ➡ keep graphics simple – but they need not be simplistic;
- ➡ screen scrolling: keep to a minimum; ie, the point to be made should be in full view. Consider a 14-inch screen size as the optimal.

Content considerations:

➡ screen scrolling should be kept to a minimum: the point to be made should be in full view;

➡ interact with text. Where possible the learner should be able to drive their enquiry;

➡ organization of content: learner drives their enquiry, so the content must have dynamic links within the material, perhaps developed through association of ideas, concept mapping;

➡ learner progress: consideration of pre-test and/or post-test with pre-test sign-posting possible areas of learner enquiry;

➡ test items need to be multiple-choice if automatic scoring is required. Free text responses are only likely through e-mail responses being submitted by learners to teachers for assessing.

Determining the structure of the information

The statements of outcomes for the learners, objectives or competency statements must inform the development of the material. When you have this information it is then possible to construct a course presentation. Whether you are starting from scratch with a new course or adapting existing materials it is important to identify the attributes of the material and label them so you are able to create a structure for the material that the learners are able to access. Just as importantly, this allows access to information by the eclectic learners.

Security

General considerations

The spirit of the Internet is that users are explorers. The use of the Internet by the vast majority of users indicates that there is no malicious intent and that people and organizations are willing to make information available to others. The access to this huge amount of information in the most part seems to be treated in a responsible manner by the people making enquiries.

Is there, or should there be, any difference in making course content available on the Internet? If a person or institution makes teaching and learning material available on the Internet, there is an obligation to maintain that material and its credentials. This raises questions of security in that the material must retain its fidelity. There must be a mechanism to ensure that the material cannot be corrupted and rendered unusable by other learners. There is also the need to make sure that different versions of the material are not generated.

Security considerations include:

➡ access by teachers, learners and developers of course material;
➡ access to test and evaluation material by teachers, learners and developers; and
➡ access to records of learner achievement.

These considerations are handled under the following headings:

➡ course content – fidelity;
➡ teacher information;
➡ learner interaction; and
➡ records of learner's activities and assessment tasks.

Course content – fidelity

Maintaining course content fidelity has two aspects. The first is the ability of anyone to access the information in the confidence that it is the up-to-date course material. The second is to access and use the material without corrupting the content. This vandalism has an equivalent in other forms of education and training such as defacing or stealing library references. However, on the Internet there is a real fear of computer hacking. I have discussed the potential for hacking with computer systems managers. If someone can hack at course material presented on the Internet, the hacker can probably hack other parts of the system such as student records. This is not an encouraging situation, given the global nature of the Internet and the unpredictable nature of an Internet enquirer.

If you are considering offering a course on the Internet, discuss the security issues with the people managing your computer system. The use of a password is not enough to protect information that has commercial benefit.

One potential answer to security of information is to have the learner download the course information they need. This effectively means that the learner is now responsible for any corruption of the information. There is also an added advantage that when the learner makes any submission back, the returned information can be quarantined from the original source. This allows verification and places the learner is a closed-user group. Such seemingly simple solutions do have overheads in computing time. This may also eliminate the possibility of the learner by default working on versions of the course other than the currently sanctioned version, which is a real possibility. In downloading a version of a course the learner could assume that this is the latest version. However, if the learner spends any length of time working on that version they may be unaware of any updating of course information. It is an expectation that when the communication process available through the Internet is used, feedback from learners will lead to frequent updating of material. As a result, different learners, working at their own pace, could end up working on different versions of the same course because they were downloaded at different points in time.

Teacher information

In transferring courses to the Internet the assumption is that your purpose is the re-engineering of the course content from an existing course. A further assumption is that the course is currently validated through the appropriate accreditation agencies. As such, the assumption is that the course material needs to be redesigned to take account of the attributes of the Internet. How are you to inform teachers about this version of a course?

Teachers will need to be informed and one way is via the Internet. With teachers on the Internet they can have their user group. Their bulletin board may even be linked to senior management. It is possible to make this relatively secure through protocol, login and identification procedures.

Learner interaction

Making the links within and between pages known to the learner

I have written above about developing a map of the information. The purpose of the map is to provide an initial location and unique identifier for each element of information and the relationship of that information to similar information or related elements in other parts of the course material. The exact nature of the identifier will be a result of you or a subject expert mapping the relationship of the information for the learners to achieve the outcomes and competencies of the course.

Then there are the possibilities of audit trails to monitor the activities of learners. In one sense this is 'Big brother/sister'. It is possible to put in audit trails of learners access to material. But to what point? If the learner is progressing through a formal course, they are responding to a course structure. If the learner is working through material in their own setting, it is the outcome of the learning that determines success, not an audit trail of screens accessed.

Structural and strategy devices for use in teaching and learning materials: Records of a learner's activities and assessment tasks

There are structural and strategy devices that will help most learners to access the elements of information in a more meaningful way. One possible structural device with the Internet delivery of course material is the use of pre-test with the result of the pre-test indicating or signposting possible areas of learner enquiry.

It is also possible to use the outcome of a post-test to provide indicators to the learner of areas of strengths and weakness. However, the Internet does not do that by itself. Like all computer applications, the Internet is only as good as the person writing the course, setting the evaluation tasks and providing the information about how the outcomes of the evaluation task should be treated.

Conclusion

To make your course material available and appropriate on the Internet requires more than the structure of material based mainly on files. A computer-file presentation has the information with a few identifiers marked to allow the user to jump forward (or back) in what is a text file. In many cases this information could be scrolled through using the down arrow or page down or holding the mouse button down on the vertical movement scroll on the right-hand side of the computer screen.

In this treatment of making information available to the learner there is little possibility of the learner generating an enquiry. The enquiry is limited to the links engineered into a file linking process by the course developer. This type of course development for use in a computer environment leads to second guessing the possible requests from the learner. If the spirit of using the Internet is to allow learners to access information, to use it and test this new knowledge and skills against their construct of the world, then access to course materials must allow for a more eclectic approach. This has implications for the integrity of the course material in isolating them from unintended or even intentional tampering. The means of protecting course materials even from unintended corruption need to be discussed, considered and put in place.

Organizing the information for presentation on the Internet through the use of a database structure increases the options for the learner as an enquirer.

chapter **7** **Cost Considerations, Economic Benefits and Budgets**

Summary

Placing any course on the Internet will involve some costs. There will be the costs of providing a course delivery service on campus, connections to students and service providers. There will be costs within a multi-campus institution and to allow access to the course material by people outside the institution. There may be costs for the learners and there may be benefits for teachers, learners and the institution. It is difficult to place a monetary value on some of these aspects. However, budgets do have to be prepared and used.

For an institution which is setting out to offer a course on the Internet, how much the institution is willing to spend to set-up the course could effect the outcomes. For example, it is relatively easy and therefore cheap to run a generic mark-up language over a Word file and claim that you have a course on the Internet (having set-up your WWW site, etc). However, in such a cheap adaptation to the Internet, learners using the course are likely to be faced with long, scrolled pages of text on screen or incessant mouse clicks as they scroll through pages of course information. In the long run this cheap and quick solution will lead to dissatisfaction by the learner and the material will be ignored. As such the cost of establishing the site will not be amortized by people visiting the site or taking up the learning materials. As a result the capital costs of file servers, LAN and WAN considerations and the costs of developing even the cheapest version of a course for the Internet will be hard to justify.

At the moment an Internet site can run off a fairly powerful personal computer with a modem and large disk space to handle the expected flood of enquiries and course participants. That is the minimum. More powerful personal computers and improved communications through ISDN (Integrated Services Digital Network) (digital telephone lines) may increase the performance of your site but the ultimate guide to performance will be the power of the equipment that the learner has available.

There will also be costs associated with providing a service on campus and of the access by people who have no affiliation with the institution, until they sign up for the Internet-delivered course. For the learner the costs could be minimal and associated directly with access to the course materials. However, the cost could be considerable if the learner is paying for hardware (computer, modem, etc) and connect time.

Cost considerations fall into two main areas: for the institution and for the learner; benefits are available to both the institution and the learner.

This chapter looks at a generic set of possible costs and benefits under the following headings:

- ➡ costs for institutions;
- ➡ costs for learners;
- ➡ benefits for institutions;
- ➡ benefits for learners;
- ➡ summary of cost benefits and the cost benefits for the community;
- ➡ budget considerations.

Costs for institutions

The costs for the institution fall into the following categories:

Delivery costs
Cost/benefit of making course material available via the Internet. In part this involves considering current delivery costs (on a basis of assumed face-to-face teaching) and comparing these costs with the possible and future delivery costs using the Internet.

Maintenance costs
In face-to-face delivery there is a cost of developing and maintaining the physical structures, the bricks and mortar. When these facilities are established there is the ongoing cost of maintenance alongside any need to refurbish these buildings to accommodate new courses.

Set up costs
The costs associated with setting up the Internet site should include: capital costs; cabling and connectivity costs such as software; systems management; and the costs associated with the educational considerations.

➡ *Capital costs.* An institution that has courses that might be suited to delivery through the Internet is one which has spent a considerable amount of money for the development of those courses or resources. The institution needs to decide how it might gain a return on that capital outlay. The capital cost of equipment such as computers and printers are amortized over time. But how do they gain a return from the product, the intellectual capital, through the use of the computer equipment and the intellect of the teachers? That is a different matter.

➡ *Cabling and connectivity costs such as software.* There is a conception that the Internet is free. This misconception needs to be addressed.

➡ *Systems management.* If you and your students are going to use the Internet, you will need a computer systems manager with the flair and vision to facilitate the delivery of course material through the Internet.

➡️ *The costs associated with the educational considerations.*
Educational and training courses are seen as a means of
generating revenue to cover the cost of developing the
courses and, more importantly, maintain the institution.
The biggest problem is that some people see the offering
of courses on the Internet as a way of recouping capital
outlay.

Recouping capital expended and intellectual capital

The expenditure of funds (resources) to develop a course are a
capital outlay. The return on that outlay can be determined rather
crudely by dividing the capital outlay to develop the course by the
number of learners who attend or complete the course. A further
refinement is to amortize these costs over the number of years the
course will run and the number of learners in each year. To this figure
has to be added the appropriate costs of running the course each year.
These include:

➡️ teacher;
➡️ room;
➡️ lighting;
➡️ expendable items; and
➡️ other costs.

To recoup the initial capital outlay on the course development incurs
other costs and then there is the added cost of reviewing and revising
the course to maintain relevance. Where an individual develops a
course, the issue of intellectual property rights is reasonably clear.
However, when an individual or organization develops a course using
material developed by others, the issue of copyright arises.

Copyright

One of the biggest headaches facing people placing course
materials on the Internet may well be the copyright considerations.
There is huge mixture of myth and reality. If you are using material

that was produced by someone else, you *must* obtain copyright clearance. Even if you are convinced that your organization or institution is the holder of the copyright (because everyone uses the material) you should check it out. This type of institutional usage giving a *de facto* feeling of cleared for copyright use is similar to the belief that 'If it's for education then it's OK'. In fact the copyright laws are clear on what you can and cannot use and abuse with other people's material.

With the development of the Internet there is a real possibility of the abuse of copyright. This possibility or real abuse of copyright is to be found in the nature of the Internet. The Internet is a place to roam to pick up ideas and to contribute. However, if you are using the Internet as a means of making course material available, the same rigour that is applied to copyright clearance in face-to-face materials or in other forms of presentation such as correspondence needs to be applied to Internet delivery. The issues of copyright are compounded if you are revising course material for Internet delivery. The person or organization holding the copyright may feel guarded about extending the copyright to a different version of the course.

If the copyright you seek is for a new course that has been designed for Internet delivery you may well face reluctance by some copyright holders to provide a release even for educational and training use on the Internet. This reluctance may be partly based on the media generated perspective of the Internet as an ephemeral thing that serious people do not do. In this respect there is a real clash of images of the Internet as an information source and the Internet as a site for surfing. The Internet has an image problem as a source of information. Although this could affect a learner's confidence in an Internet-delivered course, it may cause the copyright holder to seriously consider their position in granting copyright .

Cabling and connectivity costs such as software

This is a costing issue beyond the scope of this book. If you are planning an Internet delivery of a course in an on-campus setting or across campuses, then someone will need to develop the plan for cabling and equipment to make it all work. Again, you may be the person with responsibility for developing these plans. Hopefully your campus is networked, so you do not have to use a modem and a phone.

Systems management

In a best case scenario there will be people on campus or in the institution with some computing systems operation knowledge. These people are important if you have minimal computing skills. These are the people who can translate from the computer application (not your course) the 'user (un)friendly' instructions that you can only find by accident, are told by a friend or happen when you accidentally strike a combination of keys and as a consequence are transported into some operating system. It's a real problem that you need to consider. Effective systems management will troubleshoot any problems.

With the Internet delivery of courses you may require links to other computer resources or messaging such as e-mail. A person with the systems knowledge will be a benefit to your course delivery.

Costs associated with the educational considerations

This in part is an access issue. Over time the ability of all to meet at the Internet may be solved, in the short term (and that may be too long) it will be the advantaged in society that access the Internet and gain from this access. This is a moral and societal consideration beyond the scope of this book.

However, beyond the possible future costs to society there are some actual costs that learners, and institutions offering courses on the Internet, need to consider.

Costs for learners

For the learner the costs will include:

➡ any hardware and software costs to access the Internet;
➡ Internet connect costs through either a WAN or connection to commercial server such as Compuserve;
➡ there may be costs associated with connect times or online costs. For example, a local call in Australia is a fixed-rate no-time charge call. This means that connecting to a local service is a one-call cost no matter how long you are

connected. However, if the service is outside the radius of a local call, timed-call charges apply;

➡ there are the costs of registration or subscription to the course;

➡ there may be other costs associated with other materials for the course, for example print materials or a video; and

➡ there may be costs of using the mail and phone as part of the course.

Benefits for institutions

There are limited benefits for any institution in placing course material in an Internet environment. One is the possible increase in enrolling learners. It is possible that having courses available on the Internet will lead to an increase in enrolments. However, these increased enrolments will need to be serviced. So unless the material on the Internet leads to savings in servicing courses, any benefit may be minimal at best and at worst lead to an increased cost of servicing the course material.

One saving that is possible by placing the course material in an Internet environment is in the costs of maintaining the material. Once the material is in an Internet environment, the costs of annual revision and, indeed, the cost of a major revision as part of the quality assurance of the course (for example, a fifth-year life of course revision) is greatly reduced.

Further benefits for an institution include cost saving with:

➡ the 'patience' of the computer when testing and retesting learners for appropriate drill and knowledge;

➡ ability to provide simulations prior to real-world experience provides a learning environment and saves expensive equipment or consumables;

➡ segments of course offered on computer provide variety, may stimulate learners and promote positive attitudes to learning;

➡ courses in part or whole offered on the Internet may be accessed by learners at their place of work, at a local library or local campus, or increasingly at home. This will reduce (not eliminate) the need for further investment in bricks and mortar;

➡ when originating from a central source, content versions are minimized, quality is controllable and reporting, evaluation and record-keeping may be facilitated;

➡ a degree of individualized instruction is possible (particularly if the learner is able to navigate the content). The benefit to the institution arises from the learner's perception that their needs are being satisfied; and

➡ when properly developed and constructed, Internet-based learning is able to provide almost instant feedback. Here again the benefit to the institution arises from the learner's perception that their needs are being satisfied.

Educational benefits for learners

➡ ability to work on course at a time convenient to the learner improves their motivation;

➡ the 'patience' of the computer when testing and retesting learners for appropriate drill and knowledge;

➡ structured nature of computer-based materials gives learners the view of the content as a professional would view it;

➡ ability to provide simulations prior to real world experience provides a learning environment;

➡ segments of course offered on computer provide variety, may stimulate learners and promote positive attitudes to learning;

➡ a degree of individualized instruction is possible (particularly if the learner is able to navigate the content);

➡ Internet learning should provide the learner with almost instant feedback; and

➡ Internet material is available at any Internet-equipped site. This could be the office, the factory floor or even in downloaded form on a laptop.

With the development of global digital systems, phones and the ability to link these phones to fax machines and laptop computers, the need to be connected by hard-wire cabling will become a thing of the past at the high-tech end. At the low-tech end and for containing capital costs, current technology will be usable for the foreseeable future.

A summary of cost benefits and the cost benefits for the community

It is easy to see that the use of the Internet as a delivery tool for courses increases the options for both institutions and learners in the education and training environment. However, beyond the institution and the learner there are a raft of groups such as enterprises, industrial organizations, employer bodies, private education and training agencies, and other community groups ranging from grey power organizations to corrective services establishments and individuals who are able to tap into the Internet and use these course resources. How do you recoup costs through course fees? Or do you write some costs off as part of a community service? There is an argument that materials developed by publicly funded organizations (government) should be in the community (public) domain and therefore offered without fee charging. This is often related to a truism that increased qualifications lead to increased income. I can make no definitive statement as it will depend on institution/government/community expectations. However, you may need to consider funding arrangements.

If this wider perspective of the availability of course material through the Internet is taken into account, the cost of developing a course for delivery by a tool such as the Internet could be amortized by a significant factor.

Remember that the cost of development and presentation is accompanied by the cost of maintenance. This is hopefully not caused by users vandalizing the course material. The cost of maintenance is a legitimate cost to ensure that the course materials remain relevant and responsive to the requirements of users. The benefit to the community is that up-to-date course materials are available. How they access this material and gain benefit may be in the home, at the local library, at work or in centres attached to local schools, colleges and universities. Community members accessing material designed for the Internet will have access to interactive teaching and learning materials with the ability to communicate not only with a teacher, but with peers who are doing the same course. They will be creating their own community of learners.

Budget considerations

This section contains a brief description of the major items that will form part of the expenditure required to develop and maintain course materials for Internet delivery:

➡ management;
➡ course development;
➡ revising and maintenance costs;
➡ clerical; and
➡ staff development.

Management

As a continual process a management regime is needed to ensure that the ongoing and iterative cycle of course development presentation and review is taking place. This is also part of the quality-assurance process. The cost of this management process needs to be budgeted. The costs covered in this category include the costs of negotiation with potential clients and the seed funding that might be required for pilot projects.

Course development

The cost here will be associated with the evaluation of course content and the development of the scheme of information elements to form the base for course offering. This may require the following cost elements:

➡ subject expert;
➡ instructional designer;
➡ Internet/computer person;
➡ transfer and manipulation of documents; and
➡ copyright.

Revising and maintenance costs

Essentially these are ongoing quality-assurance costs associated with maintaining information as being up to date within the course as developed. At any one time this revision or maintenance should amount to no more than 15% of the materials available on the Internet. If this 15% is exceeded, a more thorough course revision is indicated. It is expected that all courses would face a major review on a five-year cycle. The costs involved will be:

➡ part-time subject expert/reviewer; and
➡ person to input changes (over time this would be a full-time position as the number of courses to be maintained increase).

An issue may arise in the revising process of the version of the course the learner is undertaking. When do you implement the revision? Do you need to alert current learners that their course materials are under revision? What about the learners who have just completed the previous version? Do they need to be upgraded to the new version?

Clerical

There will be clerical and administration costs associated with the presentation of material. There could be costs associated with word processing, graphics and illustrations, and computer-programming support for placing the material on the Internet.

Staff development

There will need to be staff development activities in the following areas:

➡ attributes of the Internet and how these might be used appropriately to present a course on the Internet;
➡ evaluation of courses for Internet delivery; and
➡ preparing staff for flexible delivery using the Internet as a tool. In particular this would consider ways in which the Internet could be used alongside other delivery

mechanisms to satisfy a learner's need or a request from an organization for education and training.

The essential need for staff development – and this may include senior staff and even politicians – is that the Internet is a tool for the provision of lifelong learning. With the notion of lifelong learning comes the expectation that learners, alone or in consultation with advisers, determine a plan for their education and training in the short or long term. The paradigm shift that this represents is one of learners taking responsibility for their own learning. This moves the idea of a course of study being developed from the perception of a subject expert to the idea of a course of study being developed from the perception of the learner. This change will require staff development so that subject-matter experts are able to respond to the requests of learners and client organizations for courses on specific aspects of expertise. Subject-matter experts will need to recognize the nature of just-in-time education and training as well as competency skill-specific education and training.

The budget consideration above (and probably some other considerations to deal with your local needs) generate a set of budget documents that consist of three schedules. These schedules relate to:

➡ estimated cost for providing courses for Internet delivery;
➡ the cost to learners of accessing these courses over and above any administration fee; and
➡ an estimate to revenue generated.

Schedule 1

Internet delivery development costs. This schedule is based on the expected costs of developing a one-semester course. It is assumed that on average the process to revise an already-developed one-semester course will take twenty working days.

Maintenance will not take place in the first year but may be required in second and subsequent years with an absolute requirement in the fifth year and/or at the time of a major review. I have set out the following chart but have not included costs as these will vary from site to site.

	Personnel (per 20 days)	Notional salary	On cost	Capital item/cost	Recurrent item/cost	Other item/cost	Total
Project management	1/5 (4 days)	Manager level					
Course development	(20 days)	Educational teaching					
Internet development	(10 days)	Internet literate					
Revising and maintenance (at a later time)	0 (at development stage)	Educational clerical		Dedicated PC and software			
Clerical	1/5 (4 days)						
Staff development	2/5 (4 days)	Educational training		Training materials		Training support (4x1/2 day)	
Total							

Figure 7.1   Schedule 1

The costs associated with revision may be offset against the revenue generated by the course fee (schedule 3). There are other costs. I have not included any cost of using a third party Internet gateway provider. The assumption is that you are providing your own web site. If you use a third party provider this may have some maintenance benefits and some cost savings. This third party provider should have Internet expertise that may save your budget. However, such cost benefits will be determined by the commitment of the provider to maintaining a quality site.

Depending on your budget you may be able to get outside expertise to help you with your material on the Internet. One aspect of the process you must keep control of is the educational and training aspects of the material. If you use external providers the learners will have costs. Schedule 2 below sets out some of these costs as a matrix. If you do use a private provider, the information and means of interaction must remain in your control and the learner's access.

Schedule 2

Learner access costs. There are likely to be three levels of cost:

➡ teacher/learner access on campus from a server with downloaded courseware (local access);
➡ teacher/learner access to courseware located at an institute level server (non-local server); and
➡ public, teacher/learner access from outside the campus/institute network.

Level of access	Access type	Time	Costs to learner
Local access on campus	LAN/WAN on campus	LAN transaction and memory overheads apply in all levels of access. At this level is it a cost to learner or to department offering the course	Course costs
Local to learning centre Off campus to institute supported learning centre	Non-local server WAN access	This may be local or time called charge depending on the external location costs to learner or department	Local and possibly distance (timed charges) between campuses of a multi-campus institution. Costs to learner that apply to the course when delivered by other methods
External	Institute server to service provider or direct to learner	User pays local or time called charge depending on user distance from site of course material	User pays upon enrolling in course. Link costs of real time connect for download and upload. Costs to learner that apply to the course when delivered by other methods

Figure 7.2 Schedule 2

Schedule 3: Revenue

Potential sources of revenue based on the increase in possible learner access

Practical courses

Practical courses are those that require theory and experience to be closely interrelated. This would include courses in the sciences, medicine, the practical arts, mechanics, engineering and agro/horti-culture.

As an estimate, the availability of these practical courses, or components of these courses on the Internet should provide a 10% to 15% increase in the availability of places on campus. In general, the figure is conservative because many courses have a heavy practical component requiring the use of dedicated training spaces, such as workshops and laboratories. As a consequence, if it is considered unwise for the experience of the practical component to be too far in terms of time or distance from the delivery of the theoretical component, the possibility of compressing a course is not as great as might be expected.

If the course is conducted at the learner's workplace, then an increase in enrolments will be greater. In this case the workplace is substituting for the campus and not causing an overload on campus facilities. As a consequence an increase of up to 50% may be possible using current resources with the Internet delivered course. It may be difficult to increase enrolments beyond this figure without overloading teachers or employing additional resources such as teachers.

Theoretical courses

When the theoretical components of the course are suited to electronic presentation and much of the practical component is suitable for computer-based simulation, an increased availability of places in this type of course could be as high as 50% to 80%. This is a conservative estimate. It is based on the computer application (running underneath the Internet interface) being able to cope with most of the routine tasks, such as test and evaluation tasks, that are currently carried out by teachers. While this reduces the demand on teachers' time on these routine tasks, it seems reasonable to expect that activities associated with electronic teaching will replace routine tasks. These interactive activities are time-consuming but are at the quality, value-added end of the teaching–learning process.

Potential generation of revenue arises from three sources:

(1)   increased throughput of learners enables more courses to be run per semester/year. This reduces the cost per learner in any one year;

(2)   increased access to course materials enables more learners to be enrolled in any one course per semester/year. This reduces the per unit cost of the learning material; and

(3)   increased access to a wider range of external learners increases the potential to raise revenue.

The balance to be determined is the extent to which the increase in available courses or places is available for unmet demand within the institution or available to non-institution learners either directly or through the auspices of sanctioned or licensed external providers.

An example

In this example and in the first two cases there is an assumption that courses have an administrative fee component. This money reverts to the administration. It is not available to the department that generates the course.

In the third case, the revenue generated becomes available to the sponsors and stakeholders as *per memoranda* of understanding or similar types of agreement between the parties.

On the assumption that a semester course to an external learner could attract a fee of £400, the following table indicates the level of possible revenue based on a pre-electronic delivery of 100 learners with:

Case 1:   10% increase in places due to electronic delivery by learner access eg the whole 10% to local access or the whole 10% to external access.

Case 2:   50% increase in places due to electronic delivery eg, the 25 places to local access and 25 places to external access.

Case 3:   a proportion of the 50% of places created are allocated across the access categories.

Learner access	Fees generated	Fee for course	Extra places		
Local access	Enrolment or admin charge	Revenue nil	Case 1 10 % increase on 100 places (10) assuming all places allocated to external category	Case 2 50% increase on 100 places (50) assuming 25 to local access and 25 to external	Case 3 50% increase in places but apportioned as follows
			Nil	25 places nil income	20 places nil
Non-local server	Enrolment or admin charge	Revenue nil			20 places nil
External	Admin charge and fee for course		10 x £400	25 places at £400 income	10 places at £400 income
Total			£4000	£10000	£4000

Figure 7.3 Schedule 3

There could be a Case 4 with a 50% increase to external learners and this would generate £20,000 of income. The revenue generated from external learners has to be balanced against the cost of revision and offering the service. Second and subsequent offerings will amortize the development costs further and contribute to the maintenance costs.

Conclusion

For an institution setting out to offer a course on the Internet, how much the institution is willing to spend to set up the course could effect the outcomes. A relatively easy generic mark-up language over a file will allow you to claim that you have a course on the Internet. In the long run this cheap solution will lead to dissatisfaction by the learner and the material will be ignored. As such the cost of establishing the site will not be amortized by people visiting the site or taking up the learning materials.

At the moment an Internet site can be run by a fairly powerful personal computer with modem and large disk space to handle the expected flood of enquiries and course participants. That is the minimum. More powerful personal computers and improved communications through ISDN (Integrated Services Digital Network) (digital telephone lines) may increase the performance of your site but the ultimate guide to performance will be the power of the equipment that the learner has available to them and the courses that are available.

There are costs associated with providing a service on campus and to people who have come from outside the institution, until they sign up for the Internet-delivered course. Just as cost considerations fall into two main areas of costs for the institution and costs for the learner, benefits are available to both the institution and the learner.

Course development and delivery arise from a need. The use of a particular technology to satisfy that need arises from an analysis of requirements. The real cost benefit is in the effective and appropriate development and delivery of learning materials that meet the needs of the learners. However, it is important to look at the costs, the benefits and the budget items alongside the educational and training requirements to make sure the educational needs are being met in a cost-effective way.

chapter 8   Developing Areas

The Internet is telephone technology. There is no great mystery about it. While the Internet uses the technology of satellites and computers, the interconnection is done using currently available modems and telephone technology. The initial development of the Internet was based on text. However, there are several areas of development on the Internet and the use of the Internet as a tool for teaching and learning that move it even further away from the use of text. These are:

- audio;
- video;
- video-conferencing;
- interactivity;
- virtual reality;
- access and equity;
- genre;
- teachers;
- learners; and
- information and research tool.

Audio

When the Internet started it was a text-based communication. The development into the World Wide Web and development tools and browsers means the Internet is capable of handling graphics, stills, illustrations, audio, animation and video. The capabilities of modems has expanded to the extent that quality FM (frequency modulated audio) is now available from many sites. This comes with the proviso that you have at your receiving site the modem and sound capability to take advantage of these transmitting sites.

The increase in modem capability particularly to 28.8K increases the speed of transmission but it also increases the possibility of interactive screen sharing. The speed of the lines and the error correction capabilities remove some of the frustration of screen sharing at modem speeds of lower than 9.6K. With the use of proprietary brands it is possible to set up video-conferencing at these higher speeds. At 28.8K there is only a small step to the 56/64K capable of using ISDN phone lines. There are cost considerations in the move to ISDN but this may not be a factor in the near future as telephone companies move from analogue (slow-speed) to digital ISDN (high-speed) technology. In the short to near term there will be a move to higher speed modems. This transition will support the possibility for real-time video.

Video

Video has been available on the Internet for some time. There have been problems with compatibility leading to a degree of frustration. A particular reason is that the Internet has expanded at such a rate without a standard being established. One result has been the emergence of several video standards. Yet there has been a tendency for some of the options to become *de facto* standards. The position is similar to the relationship between SGML (Standard Generalized Markup Language) and HTML (Hypertext Markup Language) and possibly VRML (Virtual Reality Modelling Language). While there will be an international standard (SGML) there will also be working standards, such as HTML, which change as they develop over time. With video MPEG (Motion Picture Evaluation Group), and TCP/IP (Transmission Control Protocol/Internet Protocol) are recognized standards internationally.

On an historical note there are the audio/graphic systems combining voice and slow-scan video over standard phone lines.

Video-conferencing

While these audio/graphic systems served a purpose and are still operating to facilitate learners' learning, there are now a range of proprietary brands of interactive video systems using the new mini or finger cameras. These use software compression of the video signal and display either through a computer screen or a television screen. These systems require the same proprietary brand at the receive site to ensure compatibility. This may cause a problem if there is a failure to recognize that some parts of the world run their electrical system at different rates. These different rates of electrical speed influence the rate at which television signals are generated and translated to images on the screen. So a signal generated in the USA is not compatible with a signal in Europe or much of Asia. This means that these video systems have to be switched to perform at the same standard.

Some of these desktop systems are based on, developed from or scaled down from existing video-conferencing systems. In many cases, stakeholders such as technicians and systems' sales people involved in the technology are critical of the slow-scan images of the 1 to 15 frames per second systems. These people want broadcast television standards. They fail to see the analytical possibilities that are in slow-rate television images. These slow-rate images almost approximate stop motion photography and therefore allow the analysis of motor skills. What technologists see as a limitation, education-alists see as appropriate for education and training use in skills-based areas. The other aspect of these mini camera/finger camera systems is that they are interactive. And they are not that expensive at under £500 for a send and receive set-up. These prices will come down and the degree of sophistication such as multi-point sites will increase.

Interactivity

The question of interaction in education and training is critical. Interaction is like gratification: there are three forms – instant, delayed and none. This holds for interactivity in text and audio-visual forms of the Internet.

Instant interaction is a close approximation of the classroom: questions are raised and discussion and solutions follow. However, this quick fix disguises the real interaction that results from the development of trust and respect that takes place in developing a collegial interaction. When people talk about instant interaction or response they raise the question of speed not the need for quality in the response. In this context a delayed response may contain a more considered reaction to the initial request. There is a possibility in some of the applications for the Internet to create an audio-visual file and transmit that file without the need for the person at the other end to be using their computer. This has implications when messaging over time zones.

The delayed response may arise from two separate actions. The first is the receiver's need to consider a response. In the face-to-face setting a learner will often raise a question that requires consideration. The second is the time frame involved in electronic messaging. This is mainly a question of when a learner lodges a request. The teacher they want to interact with may not be available at the time the message comes in. There could be many reasons for this unavailability to instantly respond. But using the Internet will not ensure a response.

However, if there is no interaction from the teacher in an Internet setting over a period of time there are serious considerations. When a learner signs up for a course there is an implied or real contract. Not to respond to a request from a legitimate learner is in fact a breach of contract.

Virtual reality

Given the combination of video, audio, screen-sharing and animation, there is the potential for on-screen virtual reality. This has several ramifications for education and training. There are the access and equity issues and educational training possibilities.

The possibility of virtual reality on the Internet raises the issue of the virtual classroom. At the outset a virtual classroom does not seem an appropriate model for presenting course material on the Internet. The main objection is that a virtual classroom carries with it the connotation of timetabling, formatted structure for the presentation of material and an expected pattern of progression through the course. This is inconsistent with the ability of the Internet to offer flexibility for the learners to demonstrate existing knowledge and skills. Courses developed for and offered on the Internet must be structured but in no way should the structure resemble a classroom. Institutions seeking to set up virtual classrooms should remember that many of the learners on the Internet are people with bad memories of their days at school. For these learners, access to the Internet allows them to access the material they want, often in an anonymous manner.

Placing course material on the Internet also has the implication of shifting the cost from the institution to the learner and more directly into the community. Placing courses on the Internet shifts the cost of providing places in schools and universities directly into the domestic setting, the workplace or community-based facilities. The cost of the bricks and mortar are shifted from the institutions and government to the person. It is the person who must pay for the computer power, even if rented or loaned at a subsidized fee. It is the learner who will have to pay the service provider for the connect time, so that they can study.

Educational possibilities of virtual reality

Virtual reality has an image of putting on the helmet or goggles, the body suit, with the tactile sensors and playing away in a virtual world. Currently there are developments of virtual reality applications for the Internet. One of these applications is the Virtual Reality Modelling Language (VRML). This application allows virtual worlds to be constructed. Alongside this are developments in modelling applications and animation. These will offer scope for developing educational and training packages.

The virtual world on a computer screen is similar but different. In a virtual world there are many possibilities for education and training. These could be classified as scenarios. The three subsets of developing a scenario are:

- modelling;
- simulation; and
- manipulation.

Modelling

Modelling requires the learner to follow a set of instructions and actions to achieve a desired result. It should represent as closely as possible the normal operations, activities and responsibilities the learner would be expected to carry out as a person in the position. The intention of the modelling process is to develop learners skills for day-to-day operations. The use of a mentor is similar to modelling in that examples of best practice are used.

Simulation

Simulation takes the scenario of the day-to-day but adds in factors that might happen to the learner when they become a practitioner. In a simulation the learner should be presented with the model setting. However, the potential for things to go wrong should be a factor. The main point of using a setting of things going wrong is to add to their knowledge and skills, not to fail the learner.

Manipulation

With the advent of virtual reality on the Internet there is now the potential for the real-time manipulation of objects on the computer screen. With this potential, the learner is able to demonstrate their knowledge and skills. There is a note of warning: that some learners in a simulation or manipulation scenario will try to force the parameters of the setting to extremes. In a computer-based setting this is not a problem as the parameters entered by the learner should cause the warning bells to ring. It is also better that the testers of the system do test the system in this learning setting rather than in the real world. It might be fun to enter in the wrong information in a simulation to see what happens, but this irresponsibility will not be tolerated in the real world.

Virtual reality and interactivity

The potential of interactivety offered by virtual reality and the Internet is only as strong as the interactivity through the mail, telephone or any computer-based system. The reality is that the person at the other end must respond. The respondent at the other end may be a 'smart' computer. In summary, the ability of learners to enter a virtual world has huge potential in education and training.

Educational

With the ability to enter a virtual world a learner can be presented with a scenario and work through the possibilities and, as a result of their input, arrive at a solution. This solution will probably only be a point of the learner testing out reactions to potential real-world scenarios. The same would hold for many training settings but there is a further potential for training.

Training

The availability of a virtual reality option on the Internet has the scope for training. The use of virtual reality offers learners the option of working with real experiences or focusing on specific skills. This ability to focus on specific skills is important in a training setting. In the real world a set of skills have to be applied in a training setting and the problem for the learner may not be one area, but a compounding of small errors across a number of skill areas. In a virtual reality/simulation, it is possible to isolate skill areas and analyse errors so they may be eliminated. This leads to the learner stepping through the process and gaining skills and confidence to complete the task accurately.

However, there needs to be considerations about aspects of access and equity, particularly if the connect times and computing power required exceed typical home and library computing power. These aspects of access and equity apply in the use of virtual reality or any consideration of technology to support teaching and learning.

Access and equity issues

The offering of any course may have access and equity issues. Traditional institution-based courses may have access and equity issues because of rigid timetables or limited offering. This is compounded when course material is offered using technology. The use of technology raises questions about the availability of the enabling technology to the general public and to disadvantaged groups. This is a real issue and needs to be addressed. Consideration needs to be made about the public availability of computer access, the linking to computer facilities in an enterprise and the options of presenting the material in other forms to meet the needs of specific groups in the community of learners seeking access to this course material.

Genre

In preparing this book I have tried to be conservative in my approach. Yet it is clear that developments on the Internet are moving rapidly. For example, any discussion on the use of virtual reality would have been considered by most to be a discussion for the future, yet it already 'exists' on the Internet. In the same manner, the future that is here, is the discussion of genres.

The consideration of genre as a means of organizing material is a double-edged sword. Most people are happy with a discussion of genre as it relates to works of fiction. The construct of a love story involving 'boy' and 'girl' generally follows the pattern of they meet, they fall apart or are separated and then are reunited. The adventure story sets out to have the main characters achieve a goal. Like the love story the ultimate goal is happiness. The detective story also has characteristics that might include a *femme fatale*, the red herring (false trail) and the confrontation with the villain. The point of discussing fiction genre here is to point out that the narratives developed in any of these genres usually follow a pattern. The settings in which these patterns emerge can range from the past to the future. So it is possible to have a murder mystery set in the twelfth century to be solved by Sherlock Holmes in the later years of the nineteenth century or some robotic sleuth of the twenty-second century.

If we consider the activities in an educational setting, then it is arguable that most teaching and learning activities could be classified as having genre characteristics. At a simplistic level instructional events fall into three categories: tell, show and do. This rather simple troika covers a range of activities from simple to complex activities and interplay between the three. For example, in the face-to-face setting of education and training the use of tell, show and do could fluctuate not just as a result of the teacher's plan for the lesson but as the teacher responds to clues for further telling, showing or doing that are generated by learner responses. Those of you with memories of teacher training, or current experience in competency-based teaching, will have the regime of objectives to be taught, competency to be demonstrated, and the activities, resources and assessment events to be used and worked through by the learner.

As a generalization these are teaching events. What are the learning events that the teaching events are expected to trigger? The learning events must trigger attention, must lead to assimilation of the new information, must lead to trialling by the learner of the new information to generate comprehension, must lead to demonstration of new understandings as a result of the teaching. However, the terms tell, show and do are too simplistic because they do not recognize the ask, respond and verify actions undertaken by an increasing group of independent learners.

In this setting it is possible to see the development (or more correctly) the potential to make obvious the genres that exist in education and training. Most learners will have experience of the tell, show, do and even ask, respond, verify types of actions. From a learner's point of view (though not their vocabulary) these could be considered as didactic, vicarious and practical learning events. Each of these expressions reinforces a view of teaching as tell, show and do. The expressions also open up ways in which learners are able to access material

Didactic, illustrative, vicarious and experiential

A scheme to help make rational the process of translation from course document to teaching and learning activities for the Internet.

Didactic instructional events are those where the learner expects to be provided with information. It is also an expectation that the learner will at some later stage use that information beyond a responding interaction with the teacher or as an illustrative experience. However, a didactic event could be triggered by a learner's enquiry.

Vicarious instructional events are those where the learner is an observer. It is an expectation that the learner will at some stage demonstrate that the observation has been assimilated into their knowledge, skills and attitudes.

Experiential instructional events are those where the learner is a participant trialling and demonstrating expertise.

In teaching the translation of the initial course documentation to the actual teaching situation goes through several stages. However, there seems to be a lack of sophistication at the crucial stage of translation from the course documentation to the material that is eventually delivered to learners. One result of this is that stereotypical teaching and learning activities are developed. These activities are seen as being economical for teachers to develop. The ability to recycle or force-fit activities tried in the past is possibly a saving in time for the teacher and a saving of costs for the institution. However, these stereotypical responses may not address the challenges to learners required by skills upgrading courses and the requirement for lifelong learning.

If the Internet is to be used to help teachers and learners move away from the stereotypical reaction in the translation of course documents to teaching materials and activities, certain processes and assumptions need to be challenged. These include the assumption that course documents are developed around appropriate competencies. While it is true that competencies in many areas are stable, there are areas such as information technology and the areas that information technology impacts on, where constant change is the norm. In these areas the ability to develop course materials will depend to a large degree on the skills and abilities of the teachers to keep pace with change.

Yet in many institutions there is an underlying expectation that the process of translating the content of materials into teaching and learning activities is precise. Whereas in reality there is a lack of precision caused by handing the course documentation to those who will deliver the material on the expectation that all practitioners have an equal understanding of the implications contained in the documentation. In many situations based on industrial processes, such as the appropriate use of machinery, or the need to train operators in the methodology of obtaining valid results from sample testing, a lockstep approach is required.

However, there are other areas within courses where a lockstep methodology could be a limitation for the learner. If, for example, there is the need to comprehend the implications of a variety of indicators during a process, then a lockstep methodology may not be appropriate. The learner will be expected to search through a 'catalogue' of possibilities to determine a 'best course of action'. These types of activities require the learner to have experience or information of a wide range of possibilities. The limitation is that the education and training is seen as subject specific and the skills involved are not seen as transferable. This limitation could result in restricted employment opportunities in the future.

There is a further limitation when the lockstep approach is used for courses offered as retraining, or for upgrading skills for more mature people. Mature learners already have skills and knowledge and become frustrated if they are forced to theorize or practise knowledge and skills already gained. In this situation the institution loses credibility. However, learners stay on the course to gain their qualification, but will be reluctant to recommend the course to others. Therefore enrolments fall. With falling enrolments the course is no longer viable and should be taught no more.

The challenge is to keep courses viable by being appropriate to the needs of the economy and or society. This challenge of translation of course documents into courses and keeping courses relevant seems to be predicated on a notion that having developed a course it is then a matter of selection of teaching strategies and resources. It is as though on the one hand there are courses and on the other there are teaching strategies and resources and it is a simple matter of bringing the two hands together. The matter is not as simple as that. Two aspects that complicate matters involve the users: teachers and learners.

Teachers

A teacher perspective on using the Internet is likely to include views such as: 'What's wrong with the current face-to-face teaching structure of content and organization?' 'I don't have time to handle this new technology.' 'Are you asking me to develop new materials for the Internet?'

Each of these questions reinforces a view of teaching as tell, show and do. Using the Internet implies there is a change in ownership of the construct of sanctioned knowledge.

In formal education and training, subject experts construct a view of information to be the 'knowledge' This is transmitted to the student to create new subject experts. An assumption is that these people now have the knowledge, but a question arises about their skills to deconstruct their new knowledge into elements of information that they are able to use in 'novel settings'. However, on the Internet, and with appropriate material, the learner is in charge of the enquiry process.

Learners

An existing but possibly diminishing attitude from the learner perspective is: 'Why do we have to do it (what ever it is) this way?'

Given that there are minimal access and equity problems with using the Internet as a delivery tool, the information made available to learners through the Internet (or any technology) and depending on the methodology, has three outcomes:

➡ incorporated/assimilated into existing 'knowledge' of the learner;
➡ incorporated in a unique way – this may or may not be aberrant, harmful or beneficial;
➡ perceived as new and unrelated information to the learner – this may be used by the learner or dismissed as irrelevant.

The learner, particularly more mature learners in competency-based learning, may ask some of the following questions: 'How is learning sanctioned? Can learning only happen in a formal setting? Do I (as a learner) need to have my learning sanctioned? Are teachers the arbiters? Could my boss be an arbiter of learning?'

As a developer of materials for Internet delivery you may want to consider other views of learners with different and equally valid assumptions:

(1) Does the student understand the learning environment?
(2) Learners come from a variety of backgrounds and not all of them have the same repertoire for undertaking learning tasks.
(3) To be a learner the person has skills in coping with the world around them.
(4) There are issues about the learner's motivation.
(5) Learners have some experience of learning in a face-to-face mode.
(6) Learners lack experience in managing educational and training material.

Information and research tool

While you may consider the use of the Internet for the purpose of your course delivery, there are other aspects of the use of the Internet as an information and research tool.

The Internet can provide access for learners to a range of information that is beyond your course offering but related to it. The Internet offers access to libraries and commercial catalogues. However, for learners to take full advantage of this access to information they will need to have search skills. These search skills will need to cover:

➡ the search facilities (engines) of the Internet;
➡ a focus on topics; and
➡ the critical skill to evaluate and include or discard information provided by the search.

The skills involved in these search processes are higher order cognitive skills. The search facilities of the Internet take some getting used to: the organization of the search might not result in the information you thought you were seeking. At the same time, if you allow yourself to wander off your original search topic, it is possible to find a range of interesting information but no answers to your quest. So, searching for specific information on the Internet requires a certain discipline if you are not to waste hours on a non-task search. If you are thinking of allowing learners to use the range of search facilities available, it might also be appropriate to include hints about developing search strategies. This information may prevent the learner becoming frustrated in working through their search.

The Internet offers the possibility of electronic mail, bulletin board, electronic chat, collaboration and team work.

Electronic mail

Access to the Internet should give learners access to electronic mail. This will allow them to send messages to others. There is one problem. The learners will need to know the electronic mail address before they send out messages. If you are developing a course, you will need to consider if you want your learners to be able to electronically mail each other. You will need to consider the questions of privacy, because the Internet is not a secure transmission system. So some learners involved in your course may have some objection to having their personal details such as address and phone number on a distribution list.

One means of overcoming the privacy issue is by establishing a closed-user group. With this technique you effectively limit access to electronic mail to those learners in the course. This has added benefits for the development of other mechanisms to encourage interaction between learners using the Internet.

Bulletin board

Bulletin boards are a means of making course information available to the learners in the class. It is also a point where learners are able to make comments on their work or the work of others. However, without sounding like a censor, submissions to the bulletin board need to be submitted through the course manager (teacher) to make sure that they are appropriate.

Electronic chat

Internet Relay Chat (IRC) is a form of electronic mail. The main feature is that the messages submitted are recorded sequentially so it is possible to see the development of points of view as each of the participants reacts and responds to the previous message. Again the use of a mediator (teacher) could be of benefit to reduce the potential for misunderstanding and resultant abuse (flaming) entering the submissions.

Collaboration and team work

The use of these messaging systems in reality leads to the potential for collaboration and team work. Some learners on the Internet may be isolated loners. However, if given the opportunity and encouragement, most Internet learners are active participants. The reality is that an Internet connection allows participation when the learner finds it convenient. It also encourages the learner to ask for or seek out the information, training and collaboration to satisfy their needs.

Annotation

A recent development for course providers is to allow learners to 'post queries' about information in the course. The teacher is then able to read these queries in relation to the provided information and add comments. This results in a notation appearing within the course materials. The end result is that other learners coming across this information see there is an annotation and they are able to open the annotation and see the comments. If the learner is not troubled by the course material at the point of the notation they are able to progress without opening the annotation. This seems to be useful device for course presenters at the time of updating the course material.

Conclusion

A word or two of warning

There is a possible dysfunction between placing course materials on the Internet and the notion of learners being able to 'surf' the Internet. To have any validity a course on the Internet requires the maintenance of the course and the verification of the students' progress.

My conservative approach is reinforced when I examine the introduction of other technologies into an educational and training setting. Most of these 'experiments' with technology are characterized by poor documentation, inadequate replication, discredit and finally the failure by teachers to adopt, on any large scale, the new technology.

Back in 1980 W M Gordon commented on the commercial success of television with young people and contrasted this success with the lack of success of educational television with the same people. He projected forward on to outcomes if similar strategies were to be used for satellite delivery:

> **"**Television has had at best a minimal impact upon the formal education of children. Commercial development has been extraordinary... children watching... and then dutifully demanding the cereals and toys they see advertised. Considering these extremely divergent success records within the same basic population, educators must look to the utilization of the media and not the technology... If satellite technology is utilized... without any change in the structure, role, functions and subject matter... [satellite]... will have the same impact that television had – ie, none!**"**
>
> (Gordon, 1980, p 341)

He also is aware of the dichotomy of the new technology in an old setting. He goes on to argue that:

> "The very paradox of something as twenty-first century as a satellite supporting something as nineteenth century as to-day's... school system... strikes at the very core of educational change. Satellite technology must be a support technology for education, but it must support an educational enterprise that is fundamentally different from that which exists in today's schools."
>
> (Gordon, 1980)

Gordon is pointing to the need of the enterprise to recognize the function that technology, in this case satellite, will offer. However, he is also indicating that there is a need for the institutions to modify or change. And institutions, particularly nineteenth-century institutions such as schools, are reluctant to change. A decade and a half later the same proposition must be raised about the Internet and the use of the Internet by teachers.

Edgar Stones starts to unravel the problem for teachers using technology when he addresses the underlying approach to incorporating media and technology into teaching and learning:

> "In recent times, solutions to pedagogical problems have very often been sought by the use of various types of technology. Enthusiasm for aids such as language laboratories, teaching machines, closed circuit TV and currently, computers, video-disks, lasers, multi-media 'presentations' have promised the pedagogical holy grail. In due course some of them have been absorbed into the teacher's armamentarium, others gather dust in stock rooms. None has brought the prophesied pedagogical millennium. Nor was there ever the slightest chance that these aids on their own could do so, since they all took as given the 'telling' view of teaching."
>
> (Stones, 1992, p 9)

Another reason for the lack of use of technology in teaching and learning is to do with the access to and manipulation of information and activities in the teaching and learning context that are predominantly teacher centred. Margret Bell lists eight reason for the failure of information technology (IT) to have an impact in schools (education and training).

> ➡ **"no coordinated vision;
> ➡ little or no evidence of what works;
> ➡ information is inadequate and limited;
> ➡ IT in learning is not always related to solutions of real problems;
> ➡ senior managers are not taking a strategic management of change approach;
> ➡ educators lack confidence and competence in the use of IT;
> ➡ insufficient or inappropriate equipment;
> ➡ insufficient or inappropriate software."**
>
> (Bell, 1993, p.7)

So one word of warning: there is in the education and training community a reluctance to adopt new technologies or adapt to new technologies. I see little reason to assume that the use of the Internet will be any different.

Then there is the challenge offered by the information age as against the manufacturing age we seem to be moving beyond. Eltis proposes that 'while acknowledging the significance of strengthening links between theoretical and applied learning, we should reject the notion that students can be prepared for the complexities of living in the 2000s by being certified that they are competent in a limited range of employment-related competencies (in the 1990s)' (Eltis, 1993, p.9). The transition is from learning for a job (which has been the myth of the last 100 years), to lifelong education and training. His argument is that it is the 'do-it-yourselfers' who explored the new technologies and it is people with a spirit of exploration who are the ones to benefit from electronic access and the informing and business aspects of the Internet. This is not just an Australian phenomenon. Whether it be an organization such as Microsoft or a backyard operator, there is education and training and commercial gain.

An A–Z of the Internet

These entries are written with the novice in mind as you will see from the first entry under access. They are also an attempt to demystify jargon. They were compiled in order to help you, as a course developer, to place teaching and learning materials on the Internet.

I use the term the Internet generically to include the World Wide Web. Where I have used the term WWW, I also include the Internet.

Disclaimer: Creating an A–Z on any topic is asking for trouble. Creating an A–Z for the Internet is even more difficult because it is a changing entity. The entries in this A–Z will be around for a while – but for how long?

A

Access

How do I get on to the Internet?

The simple answer is that you need a computer with appropriate software, a modem and a connection to an Internet service provider.

What type of computer do I need?

Most brands of computer will easily work with Internet applications. Therefore it is not so much a question of brand (Apple, IBM, etc) but the configuration of the computer. You need to think about your needs. What are going to be your main tasks on the computer, besides working on Internet materials? If you work in an organization

141

that has a computer network and computer network managers, talk to them about your plans. If you discuss your requirements with them, you are doing two things:

➡ You are alerting them to a possible call on the network to support the delivery of course materials on the Internet. This could cause a significant increase in activity on the network. This activity could cause other users to note that the network is not responding as they expect.

➡ You are also alerting them to your needs for information and service as a client. Through these discussions, a working relationship should be developed that benefits you and the course material, their network and the organization: you may be the first of many people seeking Internet access and development of materials for the Internet.

If you are working without support – and some Internet providers run with minimal support – then a starting point for accessing the Internet to put materials on it are the following considerations:

➡ If you are thinking of using graphics or video clips then think and consult long and hard. If you can only afford one computer, then preferably you should be able to partition the hard disk. This allows development space in one part of the partition and delivery space in the other part. This provides one level of security.

➡ If you are developing and delivering material on the same computer, people may not be able to access the material unless you have communication applications that allow access to the delivery partitioned section of your hard disc as a background activity. I do not recommend this: it will make both your development activity and the delivery slow. You actually need two computers.

➡ You need one computer for development and one for almost full-time delivery. Each of the computers should have 16 megabytes of RAM and something like 850 megabytes of hard disk as a good starting point. If you intend to use graphics and video your RAM should be double and your video and audio storage will possibly require gigabytes. But do not be put off by this: on some sites, 3-dimension animation are using terabytes of storage and that is huge. The RSN (Real Soon Now) is that memory costs will come down, while applications will become less memory hungry.

➡ The applications you will need to develop and deliver Internet material are difficult to nominate. Currently Microsoft Word offers an add-on that turns Word documents into Internet 'publications'. However, if you want to add interaction, then more sophisticated applications such as JAVA and HOT JAVA may be for you. These tools are all on the Internet.

➡ You will also need to contact the providers of Internet services in your area, or through your computer systems manager, to determine the access they allow in terms of preferred systems and the charges that you might have to pay. In the not-too-distant future, some providers will want statements of accountability to protect them from litigation by their clients.

Access by users

These are the clients or students or learners who may want to participate in your course. You will need to consider the access to computing facilities that possible learners have available to them. They may have access to the Internet, but do they have the applications to allow them to access all the course material, that might include audio, graphics and video running alongside the text?

Some learners might want to access your course through the use of terminals in local libraries, drop-in centres and community centres. You will need to consider whether your course materials allow access for possible learners using these facilities.

Addresses on the Internet

An Internet address consists of several components, usually displayed like this:

username@computer.site.country

In my case this is:

Ian.Forsyth@tafensw.edu.au

Or the protocol may see this address as iforsyth@tafensw.edu.au. In this case the address can be explained as follows:

1. Username (This is your name in computer communications) eg, Ian.Forsyth or as iforsyth.
2. the computer or computer site, eg @tafensw.
    ➡ com (or co in the UK) (this means that it is a commercial site)
    ➡ edu (this means it is an educational site)
    ➡ net (this means it is a network site)
3. The last section of address gives the geographical location (country), eg:
    ➡ au (this means that the site is in Australia)
    ➡ sg (this means the site is in Singapore)
    ➡ uk (this means the site is in the UK)

Another example would be

kpinfo@kogan-page.co.uk

This is the publisher's information address. It is a commercial site, in the UK.

Some e-mail addresses that you might be able to access through the Internet have the same components but the username is a string of numbers before the @ symbol. This works well but it is not as user-friendly as the username that you can usually interpret.

Then there are the site addresses of information. These take complex forms but the expression is usually as follows:

HTTP//:WWW. followed by a string of identifiers that the Internet understands.

Accountability

Placing teaching and learning material on the Internet carries with it the responsibility for maintaining that material. This will require both human and technological resources. The human resources range from those people on help desks to subject-matter experts who update the course material and ensure that it is not corrupted.

Administration of courses

The use of the Internet to deliver courses needs to be introduced and explained to course administrators. For example, the use of the Internet may mean that students submit assessment tasks and therefore teachers submit marks outside the expected time frame. Administrative staff need to know this so that marks are recorded on to learners' records without a fuss.

Annotation, post-it notes, sticky comments

This is an emerging feature possible within course presentations on the Internet. Essentially the feature should allow a learner to send in an e-mail query when they come across some material they do not understand. The query the learner generates is automatically linked to the point of the Internet material. As a result, the teacher is able to look at the query and through the link be taken to the point in the material that generated the query. The teacher is able to move backwards and forwards in the material before they generate a response. This response to the learner is linked to their query and the place in the Internet material.

These questions, queries and annotations are available to other learners, who are also able to add their notes or comments. The end result is a mini bulletin board on this aspect of the materials.

There are two consequences or courses of action. The first involves the subsequent offering of the course and the question of retaining these notations. The second involves the evaluation of the effectiveness of the course materials and the role these notations might play in revision or how they may be incorporated into a course revision. The implications of retaining the notations in further offerings are that the points raised are not overlooked by subsequent students. However, by incorporation any importance may be missed as the incorporations become part of the standard presentation of the materials.

Attributes

The attribute question that needs to be asked is: What are the attributes of the course that make the Internet a suitable tool for the delivery of all or part of the course? What are the attributes of the Internet that make it a suitable tool for the delivery of course material? Attributes have been discussed here in earlier chapters.

Audience

This really is a client question: Who is the audience for your course and what parts of the course will be suitable to present using the Internet as a delivery means? This requires some form of check on the potential learners' ability to access and use the Internet as a delivery mechanism.

Audio

Good quality sound has been proved to contribute to learners' learning. However, like video, on the Internet there are a variety of delivery standards which may mean that learners may have to go through the process of down-loading audio-driver applications in order to hear the sound clips. This problem is being reduced as the latest computers will probably have audio and video (AV) applications capable of handling several of the common drivers as part of the operating system.

There is also the possibility of 'Internet Terminals'. These will be terminals optioned to take advantage of Internet services.

This problem of audio on computers will be solved over time as the Internet standards evolve to use a wider source of drivers. Ironically this will mean real or *de facto* standards will emerge.

B Bandwidth

This is the size/capacity of the line (the jargon term is 'pipe') connected from your computer to a web site or the Internet or a host computer (see also POTS). It refers to the amount of data that can be transmitted down the line that connects your computer to the outside world. This will also depend on the speed of your modem. Data can be transmitted at various speeds (baud rates). Broadcast television has a broad bandwidth which is why you need either fibre optic cable, satellite dish or an antenna to receive broadcast television. It is possible to transmit a television-like image down normal phone lines but the bandwidth is so much narrower that there are quality problems with the images. This does not mean that the images are not useful, simply that they are of a lower quality.

For comparison, broadcast television bandwidths are around 1.2 megabytes, depending on the country and system being used, while the highest bandwidth for video available through standard telephone lines is moving from 14 to 28 and possibly 56/64 kilobytes in the near future. Currently ISDN video is available at 56/64 kilobytes. With the new generation fibre optic cables, no one, operator or user, will have a bandwidth problem.

Bookmark

On the menu bar (at the top of the screen) on some browsers there is a click-on icon called bookmark. As the name suggests, using this facility is like placing a bookmark, post-it note or turning over the corner of a page to indicate the place in the book or document to which you want to return. In the Internet, clicking on bookmark places an electronic tag or tags on sites which allows you to return to these sites without recreating your initial search. These could be useful in assisting students visit like-minded sites or as suggested places to go to find further and related material.

As a course developer you will have to provide the site address, but you should then suggest that students bookmark the site for easier access at a later date. You should note that using a bookmark will not make access time to the site faster if the bookmarked site is popular.

Browsers

These are applications that enable you to access the material on the Internet. Netscape, Mosaic, Microsoft Internet Explorer are three examples. Currently, browsers do not conform to a standard. This means that information accessed through one browser may look different if the same information site is accessed using a different browser. The differences may be minimal or in some cases access may be the equivalent of 'access denied'.

Buttons (thumbnails)

The use of buttons are a navigational device. The most obvious buttons are for forward/backward, and quit. However, buttons should be considered as an effective educational tool. Buttons could be used to link some theory to a practical simulation. Buttons could also be used to provide supplementary information in the manner of pop-down windows.

C CML (1): Computer mediated learning

This is a nonsense term because the computer is only as smart as the programmer. The computer is only able to respond to program instructions. The computer may be the means of communication and the computer applications may assist or hinder communication. However, the computer does not actively mediate learning unless it is a response to input or a programmed reaction to an input.

CML (2): Computer managed learning

This means that the computer is being used as a tool to support the developing and maintaining of records. Through a sophisticated CML system it might be possible to assist a learner to develop their plan of learning.

Construction of a home page

Your home page is like a cover of a book. It should give an impression of what the enquirer/learner may find if they search further. Given the ongoing development of browsers, a valuable piece of advice is to Keep It Simple (KIS). This KIS rule will apply as long as you are not sure of the computer capacity of your audience of learners. If they are using slow modems on computers with slow processors, it will take them a frustratingly long time to access a home page with complex colour graphics. This frustration could mean they no longer follow through with your course.

Your home page should direct access to several features. These include course information with possible career prospects; access to enrolment; access for enrolled learners to material they have worked on. Within this access facility is access to e-mail, chat groups and the interactive parts of sending assessment tasks, query and connections to other sources.

Some educational and training sites include information on the institution, the staff and a range of hype. In many cases these are poorly translated versions of the institution's handbook and can detract from any impression of Internet awareness that the home page has attempted to portray.

Course suitability

A fundamental question any course developer must consider when the use of the Internet is proposed is: Why use the Internet? You need to ask yourself: What is it about this course or parts of this course that make it suitable for use on the Internet? What, if any, aspects of the course or parts of the course are more suited to delivery by other methods such as face-to-face, in text or workbooks?

Copyright

Copyright has been an issue in education and training in terms of the proper use of an author's work. There is a widespread belief that if it's for education, any copying is acceptable. This belief is wrong. In an era of new options of course delivery and of changing circumstances of course options being developed, the possibility of infringing the intellectual property rights of a course developer or an institution are increasingly possible.

There is a real copyright issue about importing material from other sources and presenting this material as part of course material on the Internet. In many cases, standard copyright precludes the use of material in other than its original form. You will need to seek copyright clearance if the material is to be reproduced in an electronic form on the Internet.

CUSee Me

This is one of several desktop video-conferencing systems. It uses standard phone lines, though you may need to check on transmission speeds between different phone companies or countries with different transmission standards. The system was developed by Columbia University (hence the CU) as an in-house/on-campus video-conference system. The system has had a commercial breakout and is a potential desktop video-conference standard. There are other desktop video-conferencing systems which have been developed by video and telecommunication companies.

If you are thinking about developing video-conferencing, check first with your regulatory body and the current thinking of the international advisory bodies.

D Diagrams, illustrations and images

The use of this 'graphic' material is often required in teaching and learning material. However, on the Internet the use of this type of material could cause problems. These may relate to the bandwidth, the browser or the speed of the modem.

The appropriate use of diagrams, illustrations and images in educational and training material supports learning. In the evolving world of learning into lifelong learning it is important that all aspects of support for learning are used. Currently, there are problems with downloading complex or numerous graphics and images. In the short term this may be overcome by using print or videotape options. In the medium to long term, digital compression technology will reduce the overheads of computer processor time utilization and the download time to acceptable levels.

Design of instruction: see Instructional design

E e-mail, electronic mail

One aspect of the Internet is its ability to e-mail others. For you to do this you need their e-mail address and they need yours. Fortunately when you join an Internet service you are given an address. This address is appended to all e-mail messages you send. This raises the other problem that you need to know the e-mail address of people you want to contact. In the absence of an e-mail equivalent to a telephone book, this provides one of the last remaining reasons to travel to conferences. It is only at conferences that you meet like-minded people and can exchange e-mail addresses.

Error messages

As a user of the Internet you will get error messages, such as '401 file not found'. The reasons for error messages fall into three general categories:

The site is under construction and the link to the information you were seeking has not been made by the site developer. Site developers will often issue a warning at the home page if the site is under construction and you can expect to have problems.

Sometimes you will get a message that the site could not be found. One reason is that the site is turned off or 'down' for maintenance or there may be too many people accessing the site. However, if you try a second time, the site often becomes available.

Error messages may be generated if the capacity of your provider is reaching its limits. In other words, there are too many people accessing the network and this is causing the system to overload. In this case many systems will warn off users rather than have the whole system 'crash' and frustrate everybody.

Equity

Obtaining information via the Internet has created serious equity issues, particularly regarding who has access to the technology that supports the Internet services. Some people are technology literate, with the means to access this technology. These people will become 'information rich'. At the same time, and for various reasons, many people still have limited access to the technology; there is a very real danger that they could become 'information poor'.

F

Flaming

Flaming is a term used to describe an inappropriately strong reaction to a communication on the Internet. The main problem caused by flaming is people responding critically, and perhaps abusively, to

151

another user's questions or comments. This can lead to escalating hostility and communication breakdown.

File transfers: FTP (file transfer protocol)

This is supposed to allow you to transfer files from your computer to another computer or on to the host computer (the file server). Some problems arise. The file you transfer will not open because you don't have an application. It is possible to solve this problem if the creator of the file has access and uses a run-time version. This means that you end up with a stand alone version of the file.

Find

This sounds very user-friendly but in most Internets, browsers will only find a reference in the current page (or related pages) on the screen. This means that if you are in a university home page, a find request will only relate to that page. It may be that the information you require is in the university but you may have to think laterally through your enquiry.

There are search engines (what a name): these are actually sites where the site manager have conjured up topic-related sites. They look smart and they may have found sources of information that are useful to you or your students.

Flexibility/ flexible learning

A major justification for developing and placing course materials on the Internet is that it opens up the options to learners. Flexible delivery is about providing sanctioned courses to learners in a manner that meets their current situation, employment and potential career prospects. Access and equity issues need to be considered, but the use of the Internet as a tool for whole or partial delivery of a course has to support flexible delivery. A course on the Internet is accessible by a learner in their own terms of time, place and context.

Forms

Forms have been discussed in Chapter 5. Briefly, the need to generate forms should be minimized by the use of evolving templates. These evolving electronic forms may encourage the age of the paperless office in educational and training administration. However, this will also require a change in the mindset of administrators.

Fractals

Currently, the downloading of video and graphics (see Video and Graphics) can be expensive in terms of connect time and computer memory. The use of fractal algorithms is economic because the algorithm only changes those features of the screen that change. For example, the aspects of a talking head that change will be the lips, any movement of the head or the blinking of eyes. If the background is static, this is ignored by the algorithm (see RSN).

G Gophers

A gopher is a search mechanism that is an historical part of the Internet. As such it will not transfer graphics or HTML as HTML but you can use it to transfer files through File Transfer Protocol (see above).

Graphics

The use of graphics on the Internet is currently a problem, because people are becoming used to graphics appearing on their screens from the increasingly larger hard discs and from CD-ROM material, be it games or information contained in CD-ROM encyclopaedia. Any site on the Internet will be hard pressed at the moment to be able to delivery complex graphics in the same time as the same graphics can be accessed from a CD-ROM. This is because the CD-ROM is connected to or part of the computer. In an Internet setting, these graphics have to be downloaded from a remote host. This problem can be reduced if graphics are downloaded in a file transfer (FTP) but then the question arises about the capacity of the user's computer to handle the data involved and process the information.

Help

Help functions are only as smart as the people who develop them, as are all functions in computer applications. Fortunately on the Internet there are many users who have already experienced the lack of help. As sites change over time, or by the time you read this, it is difficult to recommend sites. I suggest that you browse though a computer-specialist bookshop for further suggestions. You should also browse on the Internet.

Home page

A home page is like a cover of book: it contains a title and perhaps some image, or collage of images, to provide a representation of the course content. However, on the Internet, a home page should not only provide an indication of content, it should also provide a means of navigation not just to the content, but to the requirements of the course, assessment criteria or expected outcomes and content.

The construction of a home page for education and training must account for the public face of a traditional educational and training institution.

HTML: Hypertext Markup Language

This is often often called the daughter of SGML (see below) but in reality it is a default standard to many. The main 'problem' will be that subsequent versions will address more complex screen presentation and interaction issues and this may (will) require extensive revision of material already developed for HTML presentation.

Illustrations and images: see Diagrams and/or Graphics

Instructional design

The possibility of placing teaching and learning material on the Internet opens up another means of education and training. However, the use of any media must take account of the positive attributes of the media to enhance learning and limit the factors of the media that detract from learning.

Instructional design for the Internet must, therefore, use the interactive potential, the possibility of downloading files to be used by the learner in real time on their computer, and the option of indicating to the learner, through references to other sites, alternative sources of information.

Integrity of courses

The essential question here is how are you and your organization going to assure the quality of any course or part of a course that you offer through the Internet?

Iteration

If you offer a course or modules or units of a course on the Internet, that is an iteration of the course. As a result of feedback about the course you may decide to alter parts of it. This becomes a new version, or an iteration of the course. If this happens frequently, the course is soon significantly different to the one which was originally sanctioned and offered.

What strategies do you have to cover the certification of evolving courses and, more importantly, the upgrading of the information and skills of the initial learners?

Interactivity

Emulating the traditional classroom. The presentation of course material on the Internet as an emulation of a traditional classroom would be a costly and frustrating exercise given current technology. The see, hear and read possibilities are here. The frustration of emulating the classroom are in the need to attend a computer screen at a time and place so that you can interact with a teacher.

A different version of interaction has the learner interacting with teaching and learning materials. This interactivity is my concern: the interactivity with and inside the course materials being delivered via the Internet and the teaching and learning strategies incorporated in the material. In other words: What is the learner to do? How will the learner use the material and demonstrate their competence?

J

JAVA/HOT JAVA

This is currently one of the tools on the Internet which is being used by developers to create information for the Internet, or more specifically the WWW. The ability to handle graphics and animation are the main attributes of this *de facto* standard.

Just-in-time

One of the most appropriate uses of the Internet is to deliver educational and training material as the learner needs it, or just-in-time. This delivery may be just after the learner needs it. However, for you to be able to deliver just-in-time material requires planning and preparation.

At an enterprise level it is possible to anticipate that certain training needs will arise and will probably need to be repeated in any one year as a result of retirement and recruitment. As more organizations move to computer-based transactions, the potential for computer-based training has been suggested. However, computer-based training is not highly rated or accepted as a training tool. It will be important for course developers using the Internet to make sure their course material is appropriate for the learner's educational and training needs.

This planning and preparation will enable you to cope with the expected. How will you cope with the unexpected need for just-in-time education and training?

K

Knowledge

Any course expects their learners to increase their knowledge. This can be tested through assessment tasks that determine if the knowledge has been assimilated. However, a further test may need to be applied: whether the knowledge can be used in other settings.

While knowledge has a value in its own right, the ability to apply it in a variety of appropriate settings indicates that the learner has assimilated the knowledge into a working frame of reference.

L

Learning strategies

There are learning materials on the Internet but some of these are little more than electronic versions of distance education texts. Most of these materials show little regard for using the attributes of the Internet. The principal learning strategy for the use of the Internet is the potential for a course developer or designer to indicate information to a learner and embellish on that information either as a comment or as a pathway to further related information.

Qualitative measures can be applied. The focus question in most cases is: What is the requirement of the course that makes the use of the Internet a part of the learning strategies?

Links

The Internet is about links. The origin of the Internet was to set up links between like-minded people, seeking and sharing information. It was American. It was military. It was science. Then it became education, information and available.

Links between people: e-mail

In the early days (ten years ago), there were things like smilies:

:-)

or saddies:

:-(

or descriptors, such as I have a beard:

:-}

If you are not aware of smilies you need to look at them side on.

The purpose of these keyboard annotations was to personalize the communication. In today's world of e-mail these keyboard annotations are replaced with scanned images of the most recent and most flattering image of you, in colour, with the possibility of voice annotations or video and voice clips as downloadable files.

Links between people and information

There is an expectation that using the Internet provides random access to information and that this constitutes learning. The links between people and their learning needs to be a more obvious process. The links between the teaching and learning material may be transparent. The links between the learner and the learning process need to be explicit so that the learner is informed of the sanctioned learning and expected outcomes.

Logo

This is not a reference to the computer program developed to introduce young learners to programming skills in a user-friendly setting.

In the context in which I use the term, a logo is a symbol that serves to identify an institution or an organization. However, a logo is a graphic element of the screen page. As such, the use of a logo takes up both screen space and bandwidth every time it has to transmitted. A logo serves a purpose at the home page and in some of the initial menu pages. Course developers need to consider if a logo is needed on all pages of course information. If it is, then the logo should take up a very small space and therefore a small call-on bandwidth in any course material

M Menu

This is one of the organizational needs and a key consideration to facilitate learners' access to the materials. The menu will form part of your home page and subsequent levels of the organization of material. On all pages, a menu will be part of the navigational devices which have been developed to assist learners. Sometimes these menus will be a 'second guess' of possible movements through the teaching and learning material by the learner. On a more general level, pages of information must be presented with the standard navigation of the browser being used.

Metacognition

In an era where the term lifelong learning is at the point of becoming a cliché, the term metacognition is being used more frequently.

Lifelong learning is not new. At one stage it was called the school of hard knocks. After the Second World War, technological change meant that a job-for-life was a diminishing possibility. By the early 1960s it was apparent that people would change careers at least two or three times in their working life. What does this have to do with metacognition?

Metacognition is a term that describes how learners learn to learn. It also indicates how course developers need to provide learners with opportunities to use their learning skills. It is difficult to make generalizations, but most adults in Western societies have had some experience of formal education. This experience, to a greater or lesser degree, will have informed the learner of how learning takes place. At the minimal level, learners will see learning as being based in an institution. Other learners will see learning opportunities within and outside an institutional setting.

A further aspect of metacogntiion is that the learner recognizes the abilities they already have that could be applied in a similar but different setting. This should lead to accelerated progression.

N

Navigation

This is supposedly what the Internet is all about. There are, however, some possible difficulties in getting where you think you want to go for information. The first of these is thinking through how someone has classified the information you need. For example, in this book I have idiosycratically chosen the reference 'file transfer' at FTP and X-change file.

Navigation… where did I find that information? There is also the problem of remembering where you have been. Sometimes this can be helped if you 'bookmark' a site (in Netscape). This will allow you to return direct to that site without the need to recreate your original search. This leads to an associated problem of too many bookmarks and remembering why the site is in your bookmark list in the first place.

Navigation and course material

The navigation of course material has a different context. Access to a formal course on the Internet implies that the learner is on a quest. The possible reason for the learner doing a search could range from totally naïve interest, to a practitioner seeking certification for knowledge and skills gained from their life experience. As a course developer, provider and, possibly, an accreditor of learning, you may wish to have different navigation paths through the materials to expedite the learners' needs.

Non-completion

In open and flexible delivery courses it is recognized that in some courses there are learners who do not complete the course for which they have enrolled. They may complete several subjects, but then they 'disappear'. One possible explanation is that the learner has achieved their goal. Other explanations range from poor course materials to learners' losing interest. By placing course material on the Internet, there is the further possibility that learners through their curiosity may find other sources or sites that provide information. The learners are able to access this information without the context of a course. These people are taking on lifelong learning.

Occupational health and safety (OH&S)

Learners working on material either in real time or as downloaded material and offline are working on a computer screen. This means that all the requirements of working with computers should be known to the learners. It is not enough to assume a person working on a computer knows which correct work habits they need to acquire.

There are several actions you should take to be proactive:

➡ Within the content of the course, remind learners that they need to take regular breaks away from the computer.

➡ Include activities that are not computer based but obviously add to the development of the learners' skills and knowledge at this point in their study.
➡ Reinforce the need for workplace safety This includes a range of possibilities such as the use of power-point adaptors, extension cables, not drinking tea or coffee over the keyboard, not using telephones during electrical storms, not using mobile phones (even hands-free) while they drive a vehicle.

Optimal

In the best of all educational and training worlds, there would be no need for the optimal presentation of course materials. The reality is that spending on education requires funding. Using the Internet has the potential to provide optimal access to education and training.

P

Parameters

Any course delivery via the Internet must offer opportunities for both the learner and the institution. Opportunities for the learner may be in the areas of access to learning material at an appropriate time for the learner. Opportunities for the institution include enlarging the audience for the courses it offers.

To develop materials for Internet delivery you will need to consider the following questions and options.

➡ Do the attributes of a course or section of a course indicate that the use of the Internet is warranted? This is related to client and delivery options. You need to identify (a) the clients of a course; and (b) the clients' needs.
➡ What are the attributes of the Internet that enhance the delivery of the course via the Internet?

Another important concern is the experience of the learners. Learners with prior experience in many subject areas may not need a full course. What are the parameters to be used within the formal course structure to determine a particular learner's needs? This opens up questions of prior learning, certification and the maintenance of education and training standards These are issues that you will need to address in relation to your course offering on the Internet.

Pipe

This is the jargon term for capability of the current technology to handle the bandwidth required by some Internet-related technology. For example, currently, broadcast standard television requires about 1.2 megabyte of bandwidth. Some people in the education and training community demand that this broadband service is the minimal requirement for education and training.

In my opinion the requirement for such a broadband is nonsense. There are already narrowband services such as ISDN or the compressed telematics services that provide effective, adequate and economical interactive education and training for learners.

POTS (plain old telephone system)

This relates to how you can effectively use the available communications technology to provide an effective infrastructure. It requires a recognition that high-tech systems are not globally available and that a selection from available technologies may call on the use of post (at the least), radio (in combination with post), and at best post, radio and telephone to help learners to learn.

Q Quality

This is a real issue when presenting material on the Internet. How do you put in place a certification process to assure clients and stakeholders that an Internet-delivered course has the same integrity as a course being delivered face-to-face? The issue is really one of the transition from an old paradigm of the classroom or workshop to the new paradigm of learner-centred learning.

Questions

Elsewhere in this book the need to ask questions and assess learners' answers are raised. If you are using the Internet there are issues of security about the questions as they are transmitted to the learner and the security of the learners' responses.

Then there are the questions themselves. How are they developed? How is the validity of the questions determined? How is the reliability of the questions determined in relation to the expected outcomes of the course?

R

Refresh

Often when you access a site, the resulting screen looks 'wrong'. The text may look out of alignment and there may be random images that don't make sense. This is probably caused by faults in transmission. If there is a refresh button on the browser, click on it and your screen will be refreshed. In other words the original material will be retransmitted, this time possibly with better fidelity. You will need to inform students of this function. Some will be aware of it, but it is particularly important if there are buttons and thumbnails that learners need to see.

Resources

This is the term used to describe the material that institutions are currently placing on the Internet. This information usually comprises a 'designer' home page, while the bulk of the material behind the home page is straight text 'dumped' into an HTML application with at best a few links between some key words. If this sounds cynical it is not. It is the reality because computing departments and subject areas do not have the resources to do it any other way, unless they use free-of-charge students who are working on projects.

Registration or recognition of the course

The purpose of this book is to enable and encourage course developers to place teaching and learning materials on the Internet. Some courses could be delivered to a greater or lesser extent using the

Internet as a delivery tool with only the recognition of the course provider. The status of and award from such a course would ultimately rest within the community of the Internet and the subject experts associating on the Internet.

Other courses offered to a greater or lesser extent on the Internet will have a more formal status. This requires sanctioning at two levels. The first is that of the content, the second is on the means of delivery. Without a history of course delivery, the Internet is still an exploration. However, the Internet has status. Is status a reason for placing teaching and learning materials on the Internet?

RSN (real soon now)

The computing industry and the Internet as a computer-based industry is full of promises. If you are contemplating a venture into Internet delivery then you must do it with all your wits about you. Your current advice might just be out of date, or overly optimistic.

S Screen design

With browsers such as Netscape and Mosaic there are certain default settings that in part make a lengthy discussion of screen design unnecessary. These browsers allow the display of a limited set of attributes on a screen. This will change over time. In the interim, much of what has been researched on screen design with the computer-based presentation of course material applies for presenting material on the Internet.

However several observations may help.

➡ *Home page design*. Many organizations have an impressive home page/front page. It only takes a little exploration into these sites to see that similar design considerations are not applied to subsequent information.

➡ *Extensive use of graphics and illustrations*. Serious consideration needs to be applied to the use of graphics and illustrations, not to mention video. Until fractal technology and high-speed modems become the norm, the use of graphics, illustrations and particularly video will overload computer systems. In the interim we should be developing strategies to optimize the teaching–learning potential.

➡ *The use of organization logos.* Logos serve a purpose but how big is a logo in face-to-face teaching and learning materials? It will probably appear on the front, while in some training institutions it will appear as a footer (to prevent unauthorized copying). In most educational and training material handed to students there is no logo. Yet on the Internet, some institutions have templated their logo on every page. The main result is to reduce the available screen size for viewing material.

Scrolling

One of the failures of computer-based education was the need for constant clicking on keys or the mouse. An initial evident failure of the transfer of material to the Internet is the need to keep pressing on the down arrows or down scroll to reel through what is essential page-text material.

Security of material

The use of computers in any educational and training setting presents the possibility of the computer-based material being corrupted. This may be intentional or accidental. From a course delivery and learner focus, neither should occur. This requires a plan to reduce the potential for corruption of material.

Student assessment responses

This is a useful topic to follow security. If you have students who are resubmitting material electronically for assessment it means they have access to part of your computer or system. Others may also have access to it. Computer hacking once had a connotation of prestige. A computer hacker went into a program that was not behaving as designed and hacked away at the code until it behaved. Today, hacking has the connotation of vandalism and criminality. When computer systems are opened up to access there is the potential for hacking. While there is the potential to damage course materials, there is an even greater danger of hackers being able to access the semi-public mail box and, either with malice or as a 'prank', interfere with student submissions. As a result student responses become meaningless and the confidentiality required in assessment tasks is compromised.

SGML (Standard Generalized Markup Language)

SGML is an International Standards Organization (ISO) recognized methodology of electronically marking up documents so that they are machine readable. The advantage of this is that the same information can be made available through translation to other resources such as CD-ROM or into print technology. HTML is a version of SGML but there are implications for the use of browsers.

Teaching staff and change of role

If teaching and learning materials are to be offered on the Internet, teaching staff will need induction on their role in the immediate future. In the past, teachers have had to adapt to new curriculum content. With the advent of course material being offered on the Internet there is a real challenge to teachers and their role.

Teaching strategies

These are discussed in earlier sections of the book. The main concern is that teaching and learning materials on the Internet are presented with the same integrity as materials in face-to-face teaching. Material presented on the Internet will either be part of a flexible delivery process or be the content of a delivery of a course. As such, the teaching strategies will need to account for the promotion of learners learning, the logical presentation of content and the development of appropriate assessment tasks, evaluation and reporting.

The mere presentation of the content of a course on the Internet may be meaningful to some. The creation of meaning is a result of the new information being made meaningful in relation to information already understood by the learner. There are teaching strategies to help the learner assimilate new information along with the old. In preparing course materials for use on the Internet, some of these strategies could be incorporated.

Templates

Templates provide a standardized computer (or paper) outline of a document for people to fill in. A template could be an enquiry form or an enrolment form. Or it could be a format for presenting teaching and learning materials on the Internet.

Thumbnails

This are miniature versions of an image or a video clip that alert the learner to the fact that more information is available to them. In the past, the learner would need to have the appropriate software to allow these thumbnails to be expanded. The thumbnails can more often be expanded because course developers are using run-time versions of the software that creates the thumbnails. A run-time version means that you do not require a registered version of the appropriate software on your computer. However, your computer may need a certain memory capacity to allow the run-time version to operate.

As part of the screen design, thumbnails can also be used to alert the online system that a learner may want to view the contents of the thumbnail. This means that the image can be down-loaded in preparation for viewing as a background activity while the learner is reading the screen and making up their mind if they want to see the contents of the thumbnail.

Time of course availability

You may want to consider the period of time in which you have material available to learners on the Internet. If you want your course to be 'universal' then this is not an issue. However, you may also want some downtime. This gives you a break and enables you to update the information in the course material.

Time of testing

You will need to consider the length of time in which any testing procedure (exam) is made available to learners on the Internet. The main concern is that with the flexible options of the Internet, learners will need to have access to new challenges and tests to make certain they are progressing.

Transmission faults

For a variety of reasons all to do with technology, you will sometimes have transmission faults. You will usually pick these up as the screen 'looking funny'. You will not normally get an error message as these are associated with the application/browser and warn you that something is not right either with a site or a file.

Transmission faults may be overcome by using a button found on most browsers to refresh the screen, resend the information or reaccess the site. Transmission errors sometimes happen when you access a new site, or when you access a site that is under construction. Sometimes your computer has to learn that the site you want to visit actually exists. This used to happen in old versions of one particular browser – and I should ask why you are still running it. To overcome the problem you just resubmit the request to open the site. After three requests the site comes up.

U Units and modules

Many courses are broken up into units and modules, for the convenience of running the course. If a course runs over several years, an administration difficulty arises in judging the progress of a learner. If you break the course into units and modules that are shorter than the course, the progress of the learner can be judged in that shorter term. This also creates a terminology problem. When you offer a course that is the whole entity, do you then need to offer parts that are units with modules or do you offer modules that are composed of units? This decision may already have been made for you through the requirements of national curricula or the need to fit in with the criteria of accrediting authorities. If that is the case, then you must get the terminology right and be consistent.

V Video

Video is a RSN on the Internet. The algorithms that are being developed through fractal technology are contributing to the compression of video-signal bandwidth (see Bandwidth, CUSeeMe and VRML).

Virtual Reality Modelling Language (VRML)
This is a field that offers huge potential for education and training. Here I cover it briefly in terms of philosophy, education and training:

Philosophy
The ability of the learner to enter a virtual world has huge potential in education and training. There is the ability to enter created worlds. However, of more importance will be the learner's ability to develop and, through exploration, evolve a world view. This places the learner at the centre of their lifelong learning process and has them in charge and responsible for the process.

Educational
With the ability to enter a virtual world a learner can be presented with a scenario, work through the possibilities and, as a result of their input, arrive at a solution. This solution will probably only be a point of the learner testing out reactions to potential real world scenarios. The same would hold for many training settings but there is a further potential for training.

Training
The availability of a virtual reality option on the Internet has the scope for real education and training. There needs to be considerations about aspects of access and equity, particularly if the connect times and the computing power required exceed typical home and library computing power.

If the new age is the information age, and information is digital, then training for work in those fields need not be virtual. Training can take place with real information, with real results arising from actions taken in relation to the real information.

W Work

This book and the ideas in it are about learners working with learning material. In essence this comes down to working online or working offline.

Work online

This means that learners need to access the computer containing the material they want to work with. These could be learners on campus (at drop-in centres or libraries), or off campus (at study centres or at home or work). They access the material and work with it real time. On campus and at study centres the overheads may be minimal because of the use of local area networks. The cost of working online off campus may become expensive because of the time the learner requires to be online.

Work offline

This also requires the learner to access the computer and set up an online session. However, they then download (transfer) the teaching and learning materials or information they require on to their computer and conclude the online session. This process can be short and therefore relatively cheap. Assuming all has gone well in the downloading process, the learner is now able to work with the material. There is no cost of transfer of information back to the host (your) computer.

The learner works on the material They will probably also work on other jobs on their computer. When the learner has finished working with the material, and this could be days later, they reconnect with your computer (go online) and submit the outcome of their work on the teaching and learning material.

World Wide Web (WWW)

The World Wide Web is an evolution of the Internet. The question is one of access or point of access.

X

X-change of files

This is a means of quickly transferring information from your site to the user. These files can be embedded in parts of your home page and be accessed only by people under certain conditions, such as that they register as learners with your organization.

The use of File Transfer Protocol (FTP) requires you giving access to your computer to the user or sending the files to the user on request. This means that the learner and your site must be equipped to transfer files. If you are on the Internet you will have the modems but the learner may need to install an FTP.

There are security implications in both methods. In the main if people are receiving and then resending the files with answers to questions and assessment tasks, this resubmitted material must be sent to somewhere on your site other than the location of the original material. In other words, you should set up a receiving 'postbox' to accept this incoming material. This will in part provide some protection and integrity to your original teaching and learning materials.

Y

Yack and chat

News groups and educational sites have usually established a part of their site where you can join in a shared screen to exchange views. This might require some experience of netiquette. On some of the sites these yack places are called cafés. This is to distinguish them from tutorial or library areas of the site where more formal exchanges take place. In some sites, unless you are a registered learner, you may not have access to these areas.

Z

Zip-file compression

Zip-file compression is just one means of condensing files. An application called Stuff-it is another. Using file compression may save transmission time but the people at the other end can spend a lot of time working with the file to decompress it, particularly if they don't have the application you used to compress the file. They may have to go and search the net for the particular compression you used. This can be a frustrating and annoying exercise.

Conclusion

Many times in my career I have heard people talk about the use of new technologies in education and training. Often there is the phrase that is spoken as though it were a talisman to protect the speaker from criticism. The phrase is 'We learned as we went along.' In my opinion we can all learn, but for the teaching and learning process to maintain credibility the teaching and learning process needs to be thought through. The bottom line is that we cannot experiment on learners.

This book has set out some of those considerations so that course delivery on the Internet is from an informed position. The nature of the Internet is that learners will go seeking information. As a teacher, I suggest that there are possibilities for formal education and training courses to be delivered on the Internet. This course should be a result of collaboration between the teacher(s) and learner(s) (individuals, enterprises or industries) in identifying the need for a course through content, skills and employment potential. If the course or a significant part of the course is suitable for delivery through the Internet, then there are several considerations that have been discussed in this book.

For example, an Internet-delivered course should allow the teachers and learners to identify and work through the contents and attributes of a course. There are questions about how teachers and learners will relate during the delivery of the course. There are questions about how assessment tasks and reporting are handled. These questions will be resolved through considering the communications and forms that could be developed for the Internet and the consultation.

This book has focused on one means of the delivery of course material: the use of the Internet. However, I have tried to refocus thinking on to course content and the way in which courses could be facilitated by the appropriate use of technology.

In one sense this book has been written backwards. This was intentional. The hype about the Internet has been… hype. When I first came across the Internet some years, ago it was a no-frills means of communication. Now it is progressing towards multimedia and, I suspect, a commercial focus that will distort the possibilities of access and equity, meaning that the educational and training possibilities will also be distorted.

This book has looked at the educational and administration considerations of offering a course, course materials or course delivery via the Internet. There are technical specifications of the capabilities of the Internet to deliver material that seem limiting at the moment, but these will change.

The need to consider course material and the appropriate means of handling that material on the Internet opens up several issues. These are that educational material on the Internet needs to be based on an analysis of course need, the needs of the learner and the attributes of the Internet. There is also the possibility that conservative educators and trainers may raise questions about the lack of academic rigour in the courses for a learner. Perhaps this is not an issue if the learner satisfies the criteria and competencies required?

In this book I have argued that there is a need to develop courses and course delivery for learners not technology. In doing so the attributes and structure of the course need to be identified. This also requires an examination of how the learners will be able to communicate. If the Internet is to be used, I have indicated the need for a set of forms that evolve, rather than being imposed. Given that a course is to be delivered on the Internet, I have also indicated that this will mean a change in role for both the teacher and the learner.

Finally, I hope you will explore the possibility of delivering a course on the Internet. I also hope that this book will provide you with enough information so that as a developer you do not have to learn totally by the process of 'We learned as we went along'.

For further discussions we can meet on the Internet.

References and selected reading

Bell, Margret (1993) 'IT in learning', *The Computer Bulletin*, April.
This article sets out the strengths and weaknesses of the
use of computers in education and training. These are also
the potential underlying strengths and weaknesses of the
Internet for education and training.

Bruner, J (1990) *Acts of Meaning*, Harvard University Press,
Massachusetts.
There are physiological, cognitive and environmental aspects to how we create meaning (or is it 'construct' meaning?) This readable text recognizes the learning ability of
the newborn as a starting point for lifelong learning.

Davies, Ivor (1981) *Instructional Techniques*, McGraw-Hill, New York.
This is a useful text on the role of instructional design and
technology. In my edition of the book, the Internet is not
mentioned because it had not been developed at the time
of printing. However, Davies does argue for the appropriate use of technology, which is useful for developing
materials that will support an Internet delivery or prove
to be more appropriate and economical than Internet delivery.

Eltis, K (1993) 'Reworking the Post-Compulsory Curriculum:
Balancing New Needs', *ACE NSW Chapter Monograph*, Australian
College of Education (ACE), June.

Forsyth, I, Jollife, A and Stevens, D (1995) *Planning, Preparing, Delivering and Evaluating a Course*, Kogan Page, London.
> This series of four books provides a set of guidelines for people entering education and training to assist them in working with curriculum documents.

Freire, P (1973) *Education and the Practice of Freedom*, Writers and Readers Publishing, London.

Gagné, R M and Briggs, L J (1987) *Principles of Instructional Design*, 3rd edition, Holt Rinehart & Winston, New York. (First published in 1974.)

Gordon, W M (1980) 'Communications satellites and the future of elementary education', *Unicorn*, 6, 3.

Laurillard, Diana (1987) 'Computers and the emancipation of students: Giving control to the learner', *Instructional Science*, 16.

Laurillard, Diana (1993) *Rethinking University Teaching: A Framework for the effective use of Educational Technology*, Routledge, London.
> In this book, Laurillard sets out a new paradigm for teaching in a university setting. Most of her arguments apply to post-secondary and lifelong learning.

McLuhan, Marshall (1967) *The Medium is the Message*, Penguin, Harmondsworth.

Merrill, M David (1991) 'An Introduction to Instructional Transaction', *Educational Technology*, 31, 6.

Merrill, M David (1993) 'Instructional Transaction', in *ASCILITE 93 Proceedings*, Southern Cross University, Australian Society for Computers in Learning in Tertiary Education.

Mory, Edna H (1992) 'Use of information feedback in instruction implications for future research', *Educational Technology Research and Development*, 40–3.

Rogers, Carl (1969) *Freedom to Learn*, Charles Merrill, Ohio.
> In this book Rogers sets out the concept of teachers as being coordinators of learning experiences. This is important for teachers as managers of learning. However, it is important for teachers responding to learners' needs and requests.

Romiszowski, A J (1988) *Designing Instructional Systems*, Kogan Page, London.

> Sets out a schema for designing instruction. Although written before the Internet, it contains one view of instructional design that could form a basis for instruction on the Internet.

Romiszowski, A J (1989) *Producing Instructional Systems*, Kogan Page, London.

Schamber, Linda (1988) 'Delivering systems for Distance Education', *ERIC Digest*, May.

Stones, Edgar (1992) *Quality Teaching: A Sample of Cases*, Routledge, London.

> A concern for the constituents of quality teaching. Not directed at the Internet but at teaching.

Index